<u>The Manuscript</u>

Hope in the Record of our Life The true
story of a near death experience

Mike Nickols

Preface

Sherry and I are excited to share with you how faithful God is to those who have become His children by trusting Him, how every hour of darkness in our lives is having great purpose and is turning out for our good, how God longs to connect with you and me and pour out blessings on us all when we are His. Faith in Christ is what makes us His. It is not by some human prescribed behavior. We are confident He will speak to you and give you renewed hope as you journey with us.

I have crossed into my seventies, and Sherry is in her upper 60s. We got married 25 years ago. We live in the Fort Wayne area and have for all those 25 years. We both became Christians many years before we met. Before I knew Sherry, I was a significant part of pioneering two churches in the mid-80s. Those churches are thriving today under the great leadership of the original pastors.

Later, after Sherry and I were married, we founded Envision Church along with our kids. We pastored it for ten years. Envision was a non-denominational church filled with people under the age of 30. We had a compelling reason to start Envision. God spoke to us that we were to bring to Fort Wayne the passionate worship and pursuit of the Kingdom of God we experienced in the Hillsong ministry headquartered in Sydney, Australia.

All six of our children were with us in this vision and mission. Two of them had graduated from Hillsong Leadership College, Sydney, Australia. We were all changed by our four trips to Hillsong Conference. Hillsong Conference was a weeklong gathering held in Sydney, Australia. Over 30,000 people from all over the world attend each year.

There is also the business side to our life. Sherry and I have sold small group and individual health insurance for over 40 years. For 18 years, we had 16 to 20 employees and 2000 agents in 40 states. During the time we pastored, we continued to work at our Health Insurance Agency. That allowed us to pour into the church and ministry without taking any salary or expenses out. We worked full-time in the church and our business for those ten years.

I have two sisters, Pam and Jackie, and a brother, Jeff. Sherry has one sister, Karen. All of them are married; Karen is widowed. They have all come to love the Lord and serve Him in many ways. We do life with all of them and are so grateful that God has redeemed all our family. Each of them could write an amazing book about their journey with God. There is much adversity and faithfulness, and many miracles pepper their stories.

I graduated from Indiana University in Bloomington, Indiana, in 1973. I played football there for two years and was in the SAE Fraternity. I grew up in northern Indiana. I had lived in Indiana all my life except for four years, 1980 to 1984, when I lived in California. Sherry grew up in Orlando, Florida, and lived there until she was 30. Then, she lived on the east coast of FL in Indialantic for three years. After which, she moved to Indiana, where we live currently. Sherry graduated summa cum laude from The Indiana Institute of Technology, today known as Indiana Tech. This is a small private university in Fort Wayne, IN. She earned a Business Management degree with a Psychology minor.

Our family, siblings, and children have been the birthing and proving ground of spiritual growth for all of us. Our corporate family walk has had many challenges and difficulties. The result of the struggles, setbacks, and challenges has made our family more than I ever dreamed it could be.

Knowing a bit about our family is important to the story. This is my second and Sherry's third marriage. My first marriage of 23 years was to Vicki Brattain/Nickols/Kim. She loves God and lives for Him today, as does her husband, Erik. Our relationship has been redeemed such that we can share holidays and birthdays with our family and enjoy fellowship with just the four of us. The days of recrimination and animosity have been healed.

With her, I fathered four wonderful sons. Matthew who is married to Amy Herweyer Nickols. He and Amy have four children. Two that are from Matt's first marriage to Jena Thomas/Nickols/Urbaytis. Anna Rose Nickols (Lady Rose), and Micah Nickols (Moosky to me). Anna, who goes by Rose, recently graduated from Biola University in California. She graduated with honors from the Torrey Honors program. Micah attends Grand Canyon University in Arizona. Matt and Amy have an adopted girl named Everly Grace (Evie), who was born in August of 2016.

Then at 43, Amy, who was told many times she could not get pregnant, did get pregnant and had a baby boy, Oliver Nickols (Ollie boy!). They founded and currently own a successful software development company. After Matthew, Vicki and I had identical twins, Craig and Cory.

Craig Nickols is married to Kristin Fredeen/Nickols. They are the worship pastors at Harvest Fellowship, Fort Wayne,

IN. They have an adopted son, Xavier. And an adopted embryo baby, Stella. They are both amazing kids that we love with all our hearts!

Cory Nickols, Craig's twin brother, has served for many years with Destiny Rescue, delivering children and women from the human trafficking sex trade. He also travels and teaches all over the world. He has spoken for Destiny Rescue during Winter Jam all over the country and scores of churches in many states. Tyler Nickols is the youngest son. He is married to Natalie Shank/Nickols. They have three children, a son, Will, another son Levi and a daughter Jane. They are all outdoorsmen/women. They have a small farm with chickens, pigs, cows, a huge garden, and a swamp/pond with frogs and snakes! Tyler is the worship pastor at Day Spring Church, Auburn, IN.

Sherry has two daughters. Sherry's oldest daughter is Aimee James. She married to Brad James. Aimee is an RN. She and Brad both work for the same company in Fort Wayne, IN, a large Christian insurance company, Brotherhood Mutual.

Brad and Aimee have two teenage daughters, Olivia (Livi) and Avari. They attend Pine Hills church and are active in ministry there. A great thing is both Livi and Avari are big Yankee fans like their grandpa! Sherry's youngest daughter, Melissa Siren, is married to Rory, and they live in Fort Wayne, IN.

Both Rory and Melissa are faithful in ministry at Pathway Church. Rory is a pillar on the worship team. Rory and Melissa are successful business executives, as well as busy parents of two children. Gabrielle (Gabby), who attends Bethel University, plays soccer for the Bethel Pilots, and Luke, who is an amazing baseball player, will be playing college baseball for The University of St. Francis, Fort Wayne. He is meant for the Yankees, in my humble opinion!

We have always called our blended family bonus sons and daughters. And we are bonus parents! Sherry's first marriage lasted 13 years and the second marriage for ten years. So, we have each accumulated 48 years of marriage!

A Few Words About Divorce in the Life of a Christian

Divorce has had a big impact on all our family. It has been a heavy burden to bear for everyone. However, the fruit of that burden has become a blessing in all our lives. We want to give you our Christian perspective on divorce.

Divorce is always painful. No one ever goes into marriage thinking they will get a divorce. I think divorce is more an accumulation of a lot of mistakes and relationship failures rather than a single event. Many people believe the actual act of divorce is a cataclysmic failure before God and the church.

In our experience, it is the result of many decisions over a long period that were not God's will. It is impossible to go through a divorce without failing God and others in many ways. In Ezra, God, through the prophet, told the Israelites they had to divorce their foreign wives. I am sure God hated those divorces and what they did to families as much as any divorce today. Nevertheless, divorce was the necessary outcome of their disobedience to God.

While no one wants to think a divorce is in their future, the acts of disobedience we do today can set us up for that kind of failure. In 1 Kings, Solomon marred foreign wives, and those marriages led him away from God. It caused the worship of other Gods and caused his family to lose most of the lineage of the Kingdom. He, like us, put himself first. We look to fulfill our needs someplace other than in Christ. We fail to seek God and turn to Him.

Many try to call on God when divorce becomes probable. But we need to be seeking His face long before the crop is ripe to harvest. We need to seek Him about all the decisions in our life. We start drifting away, making decisions without the consultation of the Holy Spirit. We say, "there is nothing wrong; do not get all spiritual on me." Taking that text, doing that lunch, making that phone call. We say it will be fine. All the while undermining our married and family life.

Divorce is not something that just happens. The seeds of selfishness and rebellion have been being planted for a long time. Instead of seeking God and obeying, we believe the way we want to do life is the right way to do it. We do not forgive. We do not take responsibility for our own failures. Even though we may say we believe in being others-centered, the facts on the ground are often me first.

Because we are divorced and remarried, and everyone has been reconciled, and everyone is living for God, people want that result in their situation. So, Sherry and I do a lot of counseling with people in their second and third marriages. Andy Stanley says that happy couples put the other person first. That they defer to their way of doing life. That they recognize that for themselves to win, they must invest heavily in making the other person win first and most often. Sounds good but is hard to do in practice.

No matter how much it was your fault or someone else's fault, divorce and all the sins around it are forgivable for you and your ex and everyone involved in the destruction. A new day can and should emerge with the pain and trauma making everyone involved more useful in the Kingdom of God. You need not be reduced in ministry because of a divorce. The woman at the well was divorced five times, yet God used her in a mighty way!

I know divorced people can be used by God from a Scriptural basis, as well as a practical. God has forgiven me and redeemed my life. Same for Sherry and for hundreds of people that we know personally.

Some "Christians" are critical of divorced people. They see themselves above that. Yet everyone is a sinner in desperate need of a savior. We are in the most trouble when we overlook or justify our own, often secret, failures. Often, we want mercy when we are caught but prefer judgment when you are caught. And we are especially in danger when we believe Christ's sacrifice is not enough for some sins like divorce.

In ourselves or in others, God can and will redeem every mistake and sin related to divorce. He will give every divorced person who fully turns to Him a redemption of such sweet proportion that his life will be a fountain of life for others.

Having said that, I want to discuss some practical matters about divorce. I ask you to forgive this analogy in advance. Suppose you are on the New York Yankees. You and all your teammates have the Yankee organization's best interest at heart. You want the Yankees to win! You want them to be loved and to be successful! However, suppose you got in a dispute with the general manager, and he traded you to the Red Sox. You will no longer have the best interest of the Yankees at heart. You will no longer want them to win. You will no longer want them to be successful. This is what happens in most every divorce. Soon after you split, you begin competing. Competing for resources. Competing for the affection and time of the children. Competing for holidays and vacations. Competing for important decisions in the life of your children.

Such as where they will go to school, who their friends will be, where they will go to church. Players on the Red Sox naturally are not trying to make the Yankee players lives awesome. You used to love the Yankees. Now, not so much. The divorce battle makes you feel angry and ripped off. And it is ongoing. Many times, for virtually all of life. So, it becomes hard to forgive. It is easy, in our woundedness, to want to undermine the Yankees. It is extremely easy to feel the victim and cast blame. It is easy to have distance develop in your relationship with God. It is hard to see what He is doing, where he is taking you. You think, maybe this sin has put me on the junk heap of life.

Sherry and I know it is possible to overcome this. We have seen it in our own lives and in the lives of many we have come to love. The other great traumas people face may be the loss of a child, a spouse, or someone very close. Sometimes we lose our job and our career. Sometimes we get cancer or have a stroke, heart attack, or other debilitating disease.

Most people do experience some of these things. When we do, if we respond in faith, God can use it to bring us closer to Him, empower our service, and give us much deeper joy and peace. Yet no one wants to sign up for these things. We try to avoid them. And when we cannot, we try to mitigate in every way possible. Divorce is like that. The cost is much higher than people realize going in. You may think you can avoid the cost of divorce, but you cannot. It must be paid, or your true-life spirals downward.

Sherry and I kept trusting God, admitting our mistakes, and forgiving. We fought the temptation to run and stayed full-on in all our kids' lives. Eventually, after much travail, healing has come to everyone involved. There is hope for you as well.

Today, Sherry and I are lead pastors in a ministry called Arise Ministries. It is a close spiritual family for the 100 or so of us. Arise has small groups that meet weekly, a monthly worship night, and fellowship nights at least quarterly. Arise contributes to a food pantry for widows that are truly needy. Arise also supports unwed mothers who have decided to keep their babies and other needs of people who come to our attention. Aries's mission is to be the hands, feet, and heart of Jesus!

This is the most fruitful time of ministry in our lives to date. It is not fruitful because of projects or titles. It is fruitful because we are seeing God's transformational power change people's lives. Where people were once in despair, they now are walking closely with God and realizing the destiny He created them for. At the same time, we continue to make tents in the health insurance industry. We have nothing but gratitude to God for His provision for us. He is faithful!

Introduction

No matter what you have been through. No matter how much you have disappointed yourself and others. No matter what others did to you, there is hope. Hope for an abundant life filled with joy. Hope for peace, significance, and purpose. And hope that when this life ends, we will move to heaven to be with Christ and all who loved God and went before us.

Sherry and I have disappointed ourselves and others many times. We have sometimes felt betrayed and used. Sometimes it feels like the pressure God allows on us is too much to bear. Yet God has brought us through a thousand times. And in the process, has proven His faithfulness.

God can be trusted in the dark when it looks like all hope is lost when He seems silent and distant. When what we are sure what God will do and He does not do it. In those times know, He is there. He is working on our behalf. He is bringing about something greater than we ever thought of.

Trusting God when it is not easy is one of the great secrets of life. This book is about opening our eyes to see His love, His power, and His wisdom at work every day in our lives. Hopefully, in our story, you will see parallels to your story. Sometimes, the answers we seek are hidden in our everyday life. There is a great chance that because you are reading or listening to this, God wants to provide a turnaround anointing to restore hope in your life or someone you love.

This book came about because of the life after death experience I had in 2002. In that experience, God spoke to me in a very direct way. He asked me an incredibly significant question and then gave me a strong command. As is always the case with God, His few words can be life-changing. And the revelation from those few words can keep speaking into a person's life for an exceptionally long time. This is the story of that encounter and what it has meant in our lives.

Experiencing a journey to a place beyond this world is something many people desire. The trouble is, in most cases, you must die for it to happen. No one wants to sign up in advance for that! Everyone who has experienced after-life events and returned did not plan it. God orchestrated it. That happened to me in 2002. What happened was profound and life-changing. This was true for my mental and emotional outlook. But, most significantly, was the way the world changed for us.

Contents

Chapter 1.

On the Other Side of Death

Our daughter, Melissa, had a destination wedding in Miami, FL. She and her fiancé Rory decided on a cruise for the honeymoon after her wedding. They wanted the family to come along to celebrate. Most of the family and some friends came on the cruise. It was a wonderful time until I had a serious medical event on the cruise (more on this later in the book). I was too stubborn to admit it. I rationalized the pain and embraced denial. But something life-threatening had gone on while the cruise ship was in Mexico. Something that was very scary and painful. But it had passed. I should have gone straight to the doctor when we got back home to Fort Wayne, but I felt great. I did not want to sign up for tests and surgery if I felt okay. I just wanted life to go on and be like it never happened.

Besides, I was feeling quite well. I had an important business trip to a meeting in Naples, Florida, that I was to leave for the next day.

In considering whether to go, my logic was, maybe God had healed me. Maybe, what the Mexican doctors thought had happened, was inaccurate. But either way, I seemed fine and decided to go to Naples. Sherry and I flew to Orlando, where she stayed to visit with her sister. I drove by myself the four hours to Naples. I then spent four days at the La Playa Resort.

We were in meetings during the day and then had events in the evening. When it was finished, I drove back to Orlando. That night, Sherry and I flew home. The next day, we went to Kendallville, about 30 minutes from Fort Wayne.

We went to meet with our attorney about my grandmother and mother's estates. They had both passed away within a few months of each other. I was the administrator of both estates.

After our meeting, we were on our way back to our office in Fort Wayne. I had left some work folders at the house, so we drove back to the house. We had an office off our bedroom upstairs. I went up there to get the folders. Sherry decided to go upstairs with me. Suddenly, I had pain in my chest that hurt so bad, I could not move or talk. I had no idea such pain existed or that you could survive for more than a few seconds with that much intense pain.

I was frozen in a position with my arms vertical against my chest. Sherry began to try to get me to talk, and I could not.

Shortly, she called 911, and an ambulance was dispatched to take me to the ER. Approximately sixty seconds after she called, there was a knock at the door. It was an EMT who lived across the street. He had heard the call and came immediately. We did not know there was an EMT across the street. That was an interesting "coincidence." They started working on me, and Sherry continued to try to get me to talk.

Finally, I forced out two words that, were an explosion of air and no voice. PAIN, PAIN. As I said above, I had no idea that kind of pain even existed. It went on and on and on. It never decreased, but it did get worse. I was praying, "Lord, if it is my time to go, I am ready to go, but is this pain necessary?" This is a question we all ask in some way, hundreds of times in our life. We want to live for God. We want to become what He wants. We want to do His will. But is this pain necessary? We ask it about financial pain. We ask it about relationship pain, health pain, and the pain of not becoming what we thought we should become.

God spoke to me very clearly, "If you want to share in my glory, then you must share in my suffering." My reaction to that was something like, "Great, that is not what I wanted to hear." This is the reaction we all often have. We want God to deliver us immediately. We want the mountain moved; the seas parted. We reject suffering as being a legitimate part of the plan for our lives.

Immediately after that, I thought, *okay, I have got another idea. How about you overwhelm me with a sense of your presence and love? Because I thought at this point, I would sense your presence far more than I am now.*

God spoke very clearly to me again. "When Jesus was on the cross, He cried out my God, my God, why have you forsaken me? If I overwhelmed you with the sense of my presence, there would be no suffering." My reaction to that was, *Nooooo; I don't want to hear that.* When God says to us, I will not remove the pain; we do not like it. We look for how to change it. How to approach God in a different way. How to get Him to see our side. But He is much more interested in what the pain produces in our lives. The depth of relationship with Him. The growth of true character. The empathy developed for others.

Then all at once, the pain stopped. I discovered later that my heart had stopped. They had to give me the paddles three times to restart my heart. When the pain stopped, I found myself looking down on a person that I knew was myself. I was myself, but looking at myself. Very strange.

Many times in near-death experiences, people see themselves being worked on in the ER. I was not in the ER. There was not a microsecond between life and wherever I was. I was looking at myself kneeling at an altar rail. It was a wooden railing with a padded kneeler for my knees. The wooden railing seemed to be around 30 feet long. It was horizontal in front of me. The railing turned at the left end, making a ninety-degree angle, and went on toward the back of the room.

There was a large stained-glass window behind the altar. It seemed to be about 40 feet high and 30 feet wide. It was beautiful with colors of red, blue, and a clear sort of color. I do not remember any pictures or landscapes in the stained-glass window. I watched myself as I seemed to conclude my prayer. I watched myself get up and move to the left of the altar and then turn and face to the left and behind where I had been kneeling.

Strangely as I turned, I was no longer looking at myself, but it seemed I "rejoined" this person I was watching. There was a wall with three large windows in front of me now. I would say each of the windows was 25 feet high and at least 10 feet wide. They did not have glass in them. The windows were open to the outside. I was looking out the windows with no fear or emotion of any kind. I did have the strong sense that I was looking out into eternity. I was not out there in eternity, but I was remarkably close to it. It was right outside that window that had no glass in it. There was like a thin veil that was like the thinnest of screens that covered the windows. It seemed that the screen was being generated by force. You could see through it, and you could hear everything that was going on outside. But the screen shielded the full sensory impact of what you were looking at.

Outside the window was a beautiful meadow. Framing the meadow in front of me and to the right was a forest of very pleasant and inviting trees. There were a small number of animals in the meadow, one of which was a majestic elk with a huge rack. He was standing in the middle of the meadow and looked right at me.

Behind the trees to the right, I could hear what seemed to be the ocean breaking on a beach. I stood there looking. I do not remember thinking anything or feeling anything at that moment. Suddenly, a voice spoke to me. This voice was coming from everywhere. It seemed to be coming from every molecule inside of me, in the room, and out in eternity. It was coming from everywhere. The voice spoke with absolute authority. Not with anger, but no grandma's love in its tone either. It seemed like it was asking me the most important question that had ever existed. It was like the words of a judge. The voice said, *"Are you ready for this manuscript to go the publisher?"*

Suddenly, I had a lot of feelings. Sort of an "Oh my gosh" moment. It was incredibly clear the voice meant the manuscript of my life to be submitted for evaluation. I felt some fear, a small sort of panic, and I remember thinking, "is this a trick question?"

There was never a question of whether I had an option to answer. It was more than needing a breath after a long period of not breathing. I had to speak. I spoke in a somewhat fearful, somewhat anxious voice. I said well, I am trusting in Jesus. I am betting everything on Him. He is my complete hope. So, if that is what you mean, then I am ready. But if you mean, have I completed everything God created me to do, the answer is no.

I have thought much about that moment. Sometimes I am sad and a bit regretful that in giving my answer of trusting Christ, I was not surer of myself, confident and unafraid.

In actuality, the second part of the answer, "if you mean have I completed everything God created me to do, then the answer is no," seemed to come from something other than my intellect. Possibly the Holy Spirit giving me the answer.

Every day is pregnant with possibilities of fulfilling the reasons God created us. There is also the opportunity to squander another day. I do not recall ever thinking about those questions in my life before that day. But since then, there has never been a day I have not thought of it. The profound depth of the question amazes me more and more as time goes on. *Are you ready for this manuscript to go the publisher?* I so want to be. I would say I would get a C grade on my response in that moment. I did say I was trusting in Christ. I was betting everything on Him. That is the correct answer. But my lack of confidence in my answer, I regret. Next time and there will be a next time; I want to be 100% certain in every fiber of my being that my entire life and hope is in Him. Not just in theory but when all the chips are on the line. When the actual answer for my life is required of me.

Once I answered the question with, I was trusting Jesus but had not done everything God created me to do, the voice spoke again.

"Then live what you believe."

If I had a thought, it was, huh, or "what does that mean?"

Instantly I was back in the ER. There did not seem to be a microsecond between the voice telling me to live what I believed and my being back in the ER. No time to contemplate what it all meant. And certainly, no further discussion with God. It is impossible to convey the authority of the voice and the words. Just like I absolutely had to answer the question given to me in the room, the authority of the command was beyond question. It has been twenty-two years since that day. Each day I ask God to give me eyes to see and ears to hear what "live what you believe" means. Over the years, I have begun to understand the significance of what God said to me that day. Throughout this book, we will unpack the meaning.

Chapter 2.

Mike's Early Life

I was born in Fort Wayne, Indiana, in 1951. We only lived there a month, and then we moved to, I do not know where. My mom told me we moved 11 times in 13 years. My dad worked as a supervisor of a finance company. They had 27 offices in Indiana and Michigan.

The small loan business can be very tough. You must watch closely that people are making their payments. If they are behind, you have to work with them. Rewriting loans, giving them more money, doing extensions of their payments were the positive side of helping people who were behind. If that did not work, then repossessions and lawsuits became the outcome. These were ways you kept your block of business healthy.

If there was a layoff in a small town, many of your customers could not pay. In the 50s and 60s, many common laborers came to northern Indiana and southern Michigan. They were from the hills of Kentucky and Tennessee. When they would get laid off, they would disappear back to the hills where they were raised.

Finance company managers were not paid all that well. This led to temptation because of the nature of their job. They operated independently. It was hard for my dad by himself to know what was going on every day in 27 offices. Managers would sometimes help themselves to cash by making what my dad called a bogus loan. A fictitious client would be created, and the loan money would end up in the manager's possession.

My dad told me he had many managers over the years do this. No one was ever stealing it, just borrowing it for a short time. Usually, the good intentions to pay it back did not work out. This would create the need for more and more bogus loans. And then they would get caught.

When my dad had delinquency, theft, or other problems, he would often fire the manager. Then he would move there and work the office till he was sure it was back on firm footing. All the while, he was looking after the other offices. After one problem was fixed, it would be on to the next problem office. This caused us to live all over northern Indiana and southern Michigan.

We then settled down a bit in Hartford City, Indiana. Hartford City is a town of about 6,000. Hartford City High School had 500 kids. I went to elementary and junior high in Hartford City from the second grade through the seventh grade. We then moved 80 miles north to Auburn, IN. In Auburn, I went to 8th, 9th, and 10th grade. After that, our family returned to Hartford City, where I completed my junior and senior high school years.

My Dad was an overwhelming presence in my life. He was a member of the greatest generation. From 17 years old until 21, he fought with the army in the Pacific in WWII. He was part of the island-hopping divisions. There was death and destruction all around. Dad fought hard for several years seeing friends die and bringing death to many of the enemy. He had grown up on the farm.

For a project for Matt, our oldest son, we did a genealogy report. We spent hours going through the old censuses in the library in Fort Wayne. Next to Salt Lake City, UT, it has the most extensive genealogy collection in the world. We discovered that the five generations before him had all lived farming.

Going through the censuses as far back as they exist, we could see five generations before my dad. Every one of his ancestors was a farmer. The wives were all listed as "keeping house." Most of them were poor, but they had a great love of country, having served in most every war America fought. My dad or his family did not seem to have much spiritual life. Being sent overseas as a teenager into the most horrific hell was very different from life on the farm.

At such a young age, it was difficult to see with his own eyes many of the men he cared about killed and maimed. In close combat, he had to kill many Japanese. My Dad never talked about it. Only on rare occasions when he had too much to drink would he spill some of what went on in the war.

Over the years, my brother, sisters, and I put some of the story together. I was the oldest of four. I have a sister Pam who is two years younger than me. A brother nine years younger, Jeff, and then a baby sister Jackie, fourteen years younger than me.

We all have a different view of growing up under my dad. Some of that is due to our age differences, the different ways dads sometimes treat boys and girls differently. Also, we all see things through different lenses of our experience. And our birth order impacts our perception as well.

To me, my dad was very harsh, but he loved us and had our best interest at heart. When my dad came back from the war, his parents had divorced, which he found depressing.

My perception was my dad soldiered on through life. As the British say, "keep a stiff upper lip and carry on." There was no church or spirituality in any of his family. No one ever talked about God.

My Dad had one sister named Vada. She was divorced and remarried to a man named Jack Crain. One evening at dinner, he choked on a piece of meat and died. I remember the funeral well. There was complete hopelessness. Wailing and despair was everywhere. My aunt threw herself into his coffin during the service. It was a very traumatic experience for me as a young boy. That seemed to characterize my dad's world. Yet, he was determined to have a different life.

I knew a lot of WWII veterans. Most men of my dad's generation had fought in WWII. They all had an inspired grit and determination to make something of themselves. That grit was applied to their kids in a big way. Some of my dad's favorite sayings were, "If you are not willing to die for your cause, give up because I am." "You will make something of your life (as a command, not an encouragement)." "Do not even entertain the thought of failure" and "you will graduate from college."

When we lived in Hartford City, Indiana, he was on the road, as he called it. Besides having the 27 offices in small towns, the finance company had a home office in Hartford City. Dad was still running the finance company, but we had stopped moving around so much. He now worked out of the home office and traveled weekly to the various offices. He would most often leave on Sunday night and return on Friday night. Then he would work a half day in the home office and drink heavily on Friday and Saturday nights.

In those days, he never admitted pain or struggled in anyway. He kept it in. I am sure it had something to do with the fact that the entire nation had been traumatized by the war. How many WW II vets had PTSD? Millions, I am sure. But he just sucked it up and went on. I am sure that is why he drank. So much pain.

One story that defined my relationship with my dad shaped the early direction of my life. It came my freshman year in high school. We were living in Auburn, Indiana, which is northern Indiana. Dad was on the road, and football practice had begun. I don't remember what the issue was, but I got upset and quit the football team. It was Wednesday.

On Thursday, my dad got back in town early. He never came back home before Friday. I am sure it was because my mom told him I had quit the team. He never said a word to me. He grabbed me by the shirt collar, threw me in the car, and drove me to football practice. He then grabbed me again by the collar, took me to the coach, and said, "Coach, there has been a misunderstanding. Mike did not quit the football team. In fact, he is here to tell you he will give 100% to make your program the best program in the state. Isn't that true, Mike?" Those were the first words he spoke in my presence after arriving back in town. I did stay on the football team, and it became one of my great passions in life.

Spirituality, God, and church were complete non-issues in my life. It seemed that they never came up. My mom was quiet, always in the shadow of my dad. She has raised Lutheran and had me baptized as an infant. I was later baptized as a Methodist. And later still, my aunt took me to be baptized by immersion in the United Brethren Church. It is hard to know the impact being baptized had on my future. It does say my mom believed in God and wanted me to be His. That was my heritage. I followed in the footsteps of the generations before me.

As a teenager, my life became sports, chasing girls, being in the cool crowd, and avoiding conflict with my dad. Avoiding conflict with my dad was not easy, especially when he was drinking, which was pretty much all the time. At 16, something happened that I did not understand. My Dad came home early after a road trip. He had not been drinking and didn't start drinking when he got home. Instead, he went with some guys to a Billy Graham crusade. It was an event at the high school showing a movie about a Billy Graham crusade. He went forward at the altar call and said he became a Christian. Not having hardly any experience with Christians, I did not know what it meant. He quit drinking immediately.

I did not notice any less intensity or easing up on me, though. In fact, he now wanted "family time" all the time, which cramped my style. I was not about to give up my lifestyle. So, managing the relationship with my dad was difficult.

The one thing that helped the relationship was athletics. I became successful in football and baseball in high school. That made my dad proud and gave me some space to maneuver. I was a "good kid" in town because I had a reputation of working extremely hard in sports. High school sports were one of the main pillars of the community. Many small towns in Indiana had high school athletics as a community pillar.

If you saw the movie Hoosiers, that gives a good picture of what it was like. My success in sports caused a lot of people to overlook a lot of my serious flaws. I smoked, drank, had a very foul mouth, and was a menace to girls. Only the heavy-handedness of my dad kept me from getting completely off the ranch.

Somehow the mix of my dad's discipline, overbearing as it was, and my mom's understanding ways ended up giving me some level of where the lines were drawn. I remember one time a friend named Randy and I were driving outside Hartford City. We were on a winding country road. A new Cadillac passed us, and Randy said, "someday, we will both be driving one of those." I thought to myself, "I might, but you never will."

Randy never knew where the boundary lines were. We could be out drinking and have an important test in school the next day. I would at least look over the material, no matter how late we were out. Randy would blow off the entire thing. I would get a C. He would get a 0, thus setting himself up to fail the class. This happened repeatedly.

My dad made me work in addition to playing sports, so I had pocket money. I had a paper route from age nine until got a real job. I worked first at the Dairy Freeze in Auburn, then the A&W Root Beer stands in Hartford City. After that, a department store called Vals. Then a men's clothing store, and then a series of factories. I never liked any of the jobs, but I especially did not like factory work. With my dad, there was no choice; I had to have a job. I did not like his rules then, but do not regret them today. In fact, I am incredibly grateful for it. My dad was very tough and difficult on me until he died. I resented it and rebelled against it. But now, I see its value. And I see how the path he walked made him into who he was. Today I am incredibly grateful and thankful for my dad.

As high school went on, several small colleges offered me football scholarships. Indiana University looked at me for a scholarship, but eventually, they chose not to make me an offer. My grades were fair, but I did very well on my SAT. That is why small colleges were willing to give me a scholarship for football. It is a combination of athletic and academic scholarship. Even though I had those scholarship offers, I decided to go to IU. The Indiana University Football coach was John Pont. He let me play on the team without a scholarship. It was called being a walk-on.

There was a kid a year older than me in high school named Jim. He had the reputation as the coolest guy in our school. He went to Indiana University the year before I did. He wanted to be in the Sigma Alpha Epsilon Fraternity at IU, so he went through fraternity rush. This is basically a tryout for their fraternity. You go to IU for a weekend of partying at the fraternity.

Late the second night, the fraternity brothers all get together. They review all the guests and decide who they want to invite to live with them. For some reason, they chose not to invite Jim to join their fraternity. I figured if Jim did not get in, it must be a very exclusive place. SAE was known for having a lot of IU athletes in its membership. They had the quarterback, Harry Gonso, who had taken them to the Rose Bowl a couple of years before. They had the Van Arsdale twins who played in the NBA. Somehow SAE found out I was going to be playing football. So, they invited me for a weekend to "rush" the fraternity.

I went for a party weekend, and they offered me a spot in the pledge class. Once you were invited and you accepted, you became a pledge. Being a pledge was a two-semester stint as a persecuted slave. You respected the "active" members, served them, got ordered around, and harassed by them. The 30 or so members of your pledge class get forged into a sort of military comradery. I was incredibly pleased to be accepted by the fraternity. I am sure that also influenced my decision to go to Indiana with no scholarship.

So now I am I at Indiana University in Bloomington, IN. It is the fall of 1969. Football started long before classes, so I was on campus early. Today, it is extremely hard to get any traction as a walk-on. But in 1969, they still had a freshman-only team. 1969 was the last year for freshman teams around the country. It allowed me to earn a spot on the team through grit and hard work. I started every game on several specialty teams. Kickoffs, kickoff returns, punt returns, etc. I also got to play defense some in every game.

So, the first-year football was working well. Fraternity as a pledge is a full-time job day and night. The only relief was class (which I did not go to very much) and football practice. Otherwise, we had a pledge class trainer to instruct us in the ways of the fraternity. We had study table and midnight lineups, often in our underwear. We had to clean the actives room we lived in every day. We cleaned the house from top to bottom every Friday night at midnight.

Pledges are like a recruit at Marine Corp basic training. I am sure that is where they got the whole idea. An event that first fall affected our pledge class and me. When I was a pledge, the SAE Fraternity house that had been their home since after World War I burned down.

The fraternity house was quite large. It was four stories high and was large enough for 108 of us to live in. All along the front of the fourth floor building were large dormer windows. The fourth floor was what we called the "cold dorm." No heat. Just bunks for sleeping. The second and third floors were member rooms to live and party in. The first floor was three large living areas, kitchen, and dining. It had that elegant old mansion look. Ivy grew all over the outside walls. The fire started about 5 pm. I was cleaning the room I lived in as a pledge. I and the two actives whose room I lived in had to escape out of a second-story window. Smoke started billowing into our room from under the door.

We put towels under the door and made a rope from blankets to let ourselves down. It was one of those moments when you have a few seconds to decide what is going out the window with you. What do you value amongst your possessions and trophies? I took my jacket. When we got outside, the fire was shooting out of most windows, especially the fourth-floor dormers. We had no idea who might be trapped inside. It was a very traumatic experience. By a miracle, everyone got out, and no one was hurt. This was an amazing feat because often, at that time of day, people were taking a nap in that fourth-story cold dorm. It was a place you could get away from the activity and sleep. We watched as the flames shot out of the dormers while the fire department sprayed the flames. The feeling of helplessness and sadness was crippling. After the fire, the SAE Fraternity location moved three times during my time at Indiana University. This event made pledgeship even harder. But it forged us together as a team and as friends.

Basically, I loved it. It was a great sense of belonging. And I was well suited for fraternity life. I had hit the big time.

When I became a sophomore, they eliminated freshman football. That meant all the new kids on scholarship that would have been on the freshmen team were now on the varsity.

On the freshman team, I was second-string defense and first-string specialty teams. Now on the varsity, I was seventh string for everything. As my sophomore season wore on, I saw no action, not one play. Then there was talk of the great recruits for the next year. It became clear that I would not be a contributing member of the varsity squad. Two years earlier, it would have been devastating to me. Now, this did not disappoint me very much.

Football had been the main driver of feeling good about myself and having purpose in life. Being in the fraternity had been taking over that role from football. As I mentioned, we had many varsity players in all sports who lived in the house. Even though I was no longer playing football, I still had that elite athlete status in the fraternity. Two other things inflated my sense of having arrived. I had a romantic relationship with a beautiful girl from Pi Beta Phi. In my world, she was considered the most sought-after girl, which really puffed me up. Then my parents bought me a nearly new 1969 Mustang. I felt I was achieving the social status most guys in college wanted. In fact, I could not think of anything I wanted that I did not have.

Funny how you can have everything you think you want and still have anxiety and emptiness. There is a lot of pressure to maintain your place at the top of the pyramid. It is one of those strange things of life. My current world was not delivering peace or joy. And it certainly was not giving me fulfillment. Yet it seemed impossible to walk away. In the quest to stay at the top of the fraternity pyramid, I participated in every intermural sport, from flag football to basketball to bowling to ping pong. That was a fraternity value.

At IU, it was the late 60s and early 70s. Those were very tumultuous days on college campuses. Lots of drugs, drinking, promiscuity, violence, and fighting for causes. Myself and my friends participated in it all. Classes and studying were low on the list for me. Although in my clever ways, I escaped with a decent GPA. I was always looking for the path of least resistance to graduation.

In many ways, my lifestyle was a daily task to dull some unexplainable pain. Even in my heathen existence, all the wrongs I was doing impacted my conscience. I seemed to have everything someone, my age could want. Sports fame, great fraternity, prestige, girls, great car. Yet I was very empty and insecure inside. Most of my fraternity brothers hid the truth about their life like I did, behind a facade of coolness. But in those rare moments of honesty, most of my fraternity brothers felt as insecure as I did. It was very cool to be searching for answers to the meaning of our existence, but it was not cool to find the answer. Nor was it cool to ever mention that this was not the greatest life that existed.

The girl from the sorority I mentioned above was named Nancy. She was a very high-quality girl. She did not take part in the low-life activities I was involved in. I would take her home early and stay up all night with the wild child crowd.

One story about her still can unsettle me to this day. We had gone out to dinner. In a moment of transparency, she said to me, Mike, I do not like my life. The sorority is full of shallowness and emptiness. All my activities seem burdensome. How can having everything you want end up making you feel so empty? Now I felt the same way, but I could not admit it. I began to rebuke her for her being a traitor and an ingrate to our lifestyle. She was crushed and never dared to open up to me again. I still feel bad about it when I think of it. As graduation approached, she decided that I was not a good catch for a husband. So, she returned to a school near her home. There, she married someone from her church that she had known since childhood.

Although I put on a macho face, I was devastated by the loss. As is often the case, we want to fill that void. In that process, when you have no spiritual roots or place to turn, you make bad choices. Helping to fuel those bad choices was poor timing; I was on the relationship rebound and just not behaving like a very nice guy. I got involved with a friend of mines girlfriend. Their relationship was coming apart. She was leaving to finish her schooling at an extension campus. She wanted to solidify a lasting relationship that my friend did not want. Her desires and my needs collided. Because I was reeling from my emotional loss, I was very needy and incredibly open to being needed.

Vicki (my first wife) wanted to experience several of the best traditions of the fraternity and sorority world. She knew her only chance was in the month left in the school year at Indiana University. She was leaving Bloomington after that to continue school in Fort Wayne, IN. This led to a lot of pressure to fulfill the desires she had. One of those was to be pinned. This is a commitment right below engagement in the fraternity and sorority world. It involves lots of ceremonies, serenades, and dinners. It was all designed to make it an incredibly special and memorable college campus experience.

It meant entering a commitment for the future that meant marriage and a family.

I was compliant and wanted her to have her dream. I was never the leader making the decisions, although I always put on a front. This led to marriage and to four sons over the next ten years. I am truly grateful to God for allowing me to father these amazing boys. Each of them is one of life's greatest treasures.

It took several years, but for many years now, I have been grateful for my first marriage as well. God is so awesome. He constantly mixes what we consider good and bad. Yet for Him, He knows it is all good, for those who love Him and are called to what He has for them to do. Even though we were getting married, I was not ready for the life I had agreed to enter. It is always easy to blame someone else, which I have done plenty of. But today, I see the lack of depth of character and spiritual footing on my part as the real problem.

Now that I was married and out of college, getting a job was a high priority. Getting a good job when you had applied yourself so little in college was problematic. My Dad had never stopped being a force in my life. He and my mom came often to IU in Bloomington to visit. When I would return home during college break, he got me summer jobs every year. Now that I had graduated college, he intervened with his connections and got me a job at a bank. That led to a cataclysmic confrontation in my life.

Chapter 3.

Sherry's Early Life

I am a Florida native, born in Orlando, FL, in 1953, the youngest of two daughters. My parents were married twelve years before they had any children, and then they had two within two years. Mom and Dad were married almost 45 years when my mom passed away on September 2, 1984.

Mom was a hair stylist when she and my dad met. She later worked as his bookkeeper for his cabinet business, then as a telephone operator. My grandmothers lived with us on and off during my growing up years until Grandma (my Mom's Mother) died when I was ten years old, and Nana (my Dad's Mother) died when I was 13 years old.

My Dad was a custom cabinet maker who loved making cabinets for quality-built homes with special designs. He never finished high school but was quite gifted at mathematics, engineering and extremely talented with design. He had his own business for most of my life, except for a few years.

There was a recession in 1959, and my dad's business went bankrupt during this recession. We lost pretty much everything as there were no bankruptcy laws that protect consumers like there are today. Because of that, the bank just came and took most all our possessions. I was only five then; I still remember the "people from the bank" coming to take everything we had. They took our cars, clothes, furniture, dishes, cookware, etc. This happened while Mom, Nana, Grandma in the wheelchair; my 7-year-old sister and I stood by the door of our house as they loaded our belongings in a moving van truck. We watched as they carried it all out.

Every so often, my Nana would grab something out of their hand. She would say in her Marine drill sergeant way, "put that down; you are not taking that. It is a family heirloom." And they did it! Also, ever so often, either Mom or Nana would say, "girls, hold your head up, stand up straight. They can take our belongings, but they cannot take our dignity." It sure did not feel that way. It felt like they took our life.

My Dad was gone and would be gone for days on what we suspected was a drunk due to the shame and pain being more than he could bear. He did not usually drink alcohol excessively, but this time he did.

As was common after World War II, the women of the house were strong because they were home alone raising the children while most men served in the military. My Dad never served in World War II because of a medical reason. He tried three times to enlist and was rejected every time. This was such a shameful issue for him. We knew never to bring up this issue as it was a very painful subject for Dad. He was the youngest of seven children, and three of his brothers were in the service during World War II. It was the patriotic and manly thing to do, and his inability to fulfill the call of duty was embarrassing for him. My Dad's not being in the service attacked my dad's manhood until the day he died. Now, with the bankruptcy, it was another attack from his perspective. We were homeless for just a short stint due to the bankruptcy and losing our house.

As you can imagine, this was traumatic for our family in many ways. Dad (and Mom) quickly got us back on our feet financially as he went to work as an insurance salesman for Lincoln National Life Insurance. And he was very successful with this sales position. But he hated the job. He much preferred to work with his hands. After the insurance job, he worked for the Housing Authority of Orlando, FL, HUD for a few years. During this job, he started making cabinets for some friends part-time. Eventually, he returned to making cabinets full-time. Making cabinets was his calling. He made cabinets until the day he died at age 76!

Dad was a great Dad, and we were very close. He had a strong work ethic, loving, kind, funny, generous, forgiving, and was always there when we needed him. My mom was a terrific mom! She was highly intelligent, strong, the oldest of her two siblings so was a very responsible person. She, too, had a strong work ethic, and both my parents loved people.

Mom had kept my dad's books for his business while staying in the home with my sister and me, but when the business went bankrupt, she got a job outside the home. Before my mom had children, she had been a beautician, but she did not want to return to that line of work. My uncle worked for a communications company called Southern Bell. He helped her get a job as a PBX operator or a telephone lady, as we called them that day. She would plug the wires in the correct line when people placed telephone calls. This was a great job for my mom. She loved people, and they loved her.

Mom was kind but not given to her emotions like my dad could be. Mom was super intelligent too. She received a full academic scholarship for college after high school. She always regretted not going to college. But since she was the oldest of her siblings and her mom was handicapped, needing full-time care in a wheelchair, she saw no other way but to go to work to support her family. Her mom had a stroke at age 49 that left her paralyzed. My mom was only 13 when her mom had the stroke, and there were two younger brothers in the house that needed care. When Mom graduated high school, her dad abandoned the family. So, it was just a perfect storm of a calamity that prevented Mom from using the scholarship to further her education. But, this setback made her a very responsible person.

We were Christians. Almost all our family on both sides were Christians. My Dad was the "song leader," and Mom played the organ/piano for the church we attended when I was young. I got baptized at age ten, and for some reason, right after that, my parents left church and never returned to regular attendance. We never asked why, and it was not discussed, so one had to assume there was some type of hurt or offense.

I never knew my grandfathers; my paternal Grandfather had passed away before I was born, and my maternal Grandfather was not in my mom's life. As I mentioned, both grandmothers lived with us much of the time. They could not have been more different. My paternal grandmother, Nana, was like a Marine drill sergeant. She stood only 4 feet 10 inches tall. She was extremely strict, was not intimidated by anyone or anything, and commanded respect everywhere she went. She grew up in Washington DC, and her father was the Ambassador to the United States from France. She went to college and had a Home Economics degree.

Growing up with that background, she believed in etiquette, protocols, and acting like ladies. She was also a very committed Christian. Nana's Christian convictions were a constant in my life. I loved her dearly, and we were close. We did not have a big house, so Nana shared a bedroom with me. We often said our prayers together and lay in the dark talking. I loved her even though she was tough as nails on all her grandchildren. She was a perfectionistic and demanded excellence. Her mission was teaching us everything she knew. She was an excellent cook, housekeeper, seamstress, and bossy! She expected us at an incredibly young age to do it as well as she did. So, you just kept doing whatever the task was until you perfected it to her liking.

However tough she was on us grandkids, I knew she loved me. As Nana got older, she lost her eyesight; she needed care getting fed, dressed, bathed, going to the bathroom, and getting around. I was thrilled to take this assignment on during summer when school was out. My two aunts shared helping with Nana when I was in school. Nana and I had great talks. I did not realize, until much later, how much influence she was in my life. When people live together, you see the good and bad in them. There were times I really felt bad for my mom as Nana could be quite opinionated and was not one to hold back. As an adult, I have often wondered how my mom kept her cool with some of the remarks Nana made to her and others in the family. Nana was not only tough, but she was the matriarch of our family until the day she died.

My maternal grandmother, Grandma, was a very tall woman, about six feet tall. She was paralyzed from the waist down. It was a challenge to help her as she needed care for daily living. She was in a wheelchair and needed help to go to the bathroom, dress herself and get into bed. So, my mom, Nana, my sister, and I did whatever was needed to help her. My sister and I were young, from when we were born until probably around 5 or 6 for me and 7 or 8 for my sister; Grandma stayed with us. After that time, she went to stay in a nursing home. She was always laughing; everything was fun or funny to her. She was a delight to have around. I never once recall anyone complaining about helping her. No one considered her a burden whatsoever! In fact, the opposite was true.

Once we were lifting her into the bed, my mom, Nana, my sister, and I were all helping. If you have ever lifted a six-foot-tall person's dead weight, you understand why it took all of us to do it. We had wood floors. Mine and my sister's job was to hold the wheelchair until she was in the bed enough for Mom and Nana to take it from there. I was only three when this happened, and my sister was five. We somehow got distracted on the job. Mom and Nana lost hold of Grandma. Because my sister and I were not holding the wheelchair steady like we were supposed to be doing, Grandma slid under the bed. Her head was sticking out from the bed, which was high up off the floor. The bed had to be high because of her getting in and out of the wheelchair. I thought my sister and I would get it from Nana for sure. We had failed to do our job. But Grandma, who was lying under the bed, started laughing. It was so infectious that we all laughed (including Nana, who rarely laughed). This continued until Grandma said, "Go get your dad to get me out of here." Our Dad worked near our home, as he had his shop in a building on our property where we lived. He came and got Grandma in the bed. Dad and Grandma had a very special bond; they really loved each other.

Dad had an extremely outgoing personality. He never met a stranger. He had the best sense of humor. No one ever talked about hardships. I remember us all being grateful for everything, whatever we had! Their generation kept what was called a "stiff upper lip" and moved on. Maybe looking back on it, it was not the best way to handle so many traumas they faced, but it was the way during that time of life.

The generation from the Great Depression and World War II were a different people from my generation, Baby Boomers, and certainly from the generations that followed the Baby Boomers. We, as a culture, have changed so much from what they were then. At least in my family, we worked hard, and having a good work ethic was the equivalent of having a good reputation. We did not complain. We said prayers before our meals and went to church on Sunday.

I grew up from the womb up until now, in the church. In my world, women did not cuss, and they apologized when my dad or some other man said a curse word. We listened to the radio a lot until about 1959; around 1960, we got our first television. The radio program, Through the Bible with J. Vernon McGee was a daily staple in our house. Mom, Nana, Grandma, my sister, Karen, and I listened to this program together. Other than J. Vernon McGee, Billy Graham was the only preacher on TV or radio we were allowed to listen to. So, I got a good foundation of the Bible from these daily Bible studies.

My sister, Karen, kept a close watch on me most of the time, making Nana look like a tame drill sergeant. She made me toe the line. Karen had a lot of responsibility put on her to watch over me. Plus, I looked up to Karen and always wanted to be with her. Unfortunately for Karen, my parents made her take me with her when she went with her friends. This was not a good thing for either of us. She would rather me not be there, and since they were older, I did not fit in.

Karen has the typical oldest personality, take charge, be in control, and she had the bossy gene! I am sure at times, I drove her up the wall, plus she had to be resentful that she had to take me along wherever she went. Many times, I felt like I did not belong. Karen was bold, competent, and could be mouthy. She could do everything I wished I could, like cheerleading, play piano by what we called "ear." She was good at crafts and cooking, even though, as a young girl, she did not like to do them. I pretty much thought she was the coolest person I knew.

Nana thought Karen was sassy and had what we called a smart-alecky attitude. Nana preferred my compliant ways and constantly told my sister, why can't you be like Sherry? Sweet and easy to get along with. Well, as you can imagine, making comparisons is not a winner. This worked out bad for both Karen and I because instead of helping our relationship be stronger, it put a wedge in it and strained it. Thankfully, as we got older, our relationship improved, and we are very close today and all through our adult years.

The rest of my childhood and teenage years had a fair amount of not-good stuff mixed in with many great times. At around age 3 to 5, some really bad things took place, as happens to many little girls at the hands of a neighbor boy. I remember he threatened me if I told. Also, one time he killed a kitten of ours just to scare me. I was too young to understand it was intimidation. It worked to keep me silent. Years later, I shared this with my sister, Karen, who said the same thing happened to her with the same boy. I think this abuse happened quite often in the 1950s. Still, because of the culture of not talking about hardships, it went unreported.

I always loved going to church. It brought me peace and joy and lots of friends. I loved singing, and church allowed me to sing. I took piano lessons but never got good at it. Karen got all the piano-playing genes. Church overall was where I was most comfortable. I loved learning Bible verses, singing in the choir, and even occasionally would do a "special song." We lived close to a country Baptist church from the time I was ten until I graduated high school; I attended church there. In addition to church, I loved school. I have always loved learning.

As much as I loved learning, I was just an average student. However, when I went to high school in ninth grade, the school counselor called me in her office. I thought I was in trouble but did not know what I did. The counselor was an amazing person. The type of person who saw potential in everyone. She encouraged me to be a better student. She said I was more capable than my grades (which were Cs at that time) reflected. The counselor said she wanted to see me regularly and see how my grades were coming. Well, just from that encouragement alone and a lot of hard work, my grades went up almost immediately to A's. I learned then how very crucial words are to people. Being a heartfelt encourager to others can bring life to them. As kind and loving as our parents were, we rarely heard words of encouragement. We were just expected to do our best.

I was 18 the first time I married. His name was Mike. He had two sisters who I was very close with. His Dad had been in the Air Force working in communication. When we met, his Dad worked for a communication company climbing these very tall towers. His mom was a stay-at-home mom. When we married, we were both young, just out of high school, and had been dating all through high school. I had been a Christian since the age of ten. He and his family attend a different Baptist church than I did, so I began to attend with him and his family.

For some reason, it seemed like these were good enough qualifications to marry him. I must admit that God tried to speak to me about this marriage, but I did not listen. The marriage was not good from the very beginning. But, like some of you, I tried to stick it out. We both had quick tempers and many unhealed hurts. It was quite the powder keg for 13 years. We had two daughters. I truly thank God for these girls; they are absolutely God-sent! It was not good what the girls had to see and hear during those years.

As a Christian, this situation made me feel so guilty, and the devil was more than happy to add his two cents into the thoughts in my mind. I felt like a disappointment to myself, my family, and God. There were so many days that just seemed like there was no way out of this. The same strife, fighting, and terrible behaviors day after day. I was so ashamed to tell anyone, but often, the war was visible to others around us.

We had a wonderful babysitter for our daughters who went to our church. She was older than us and had teenage children. She was like a grandmother to the girls. Our family adored this family. One day after a horrible argument between my then husband and me, it was learned that the teenage daughter of our babysitter was pregnant with his child. I must confess that while this was devastating in so many ways, especially to our daughters, it did seem to me as God might be up to something. Romans 8:28 has been one of my life verses all my life, "And we know that all things work together for good to them who love God and are called according to His purpose."

Remember, friends; He works in ways we often do not expect! His redeeming processes are often misunderstood in the moment. Our marriage ended. The girls' Dad moved out on a Saturday night. Then suddenly, the very next week, on a

Sunday morning, my mother passed away. She had not been sick a day in her life; her death was totally unexpected. She had a heart attack that pretty much killed her instantly.

The day my mom died, Dad had several TIA's, which are mini-strokes, and he was never the same. He looked the same but was not the same Dad we knew before. My sister Karen and I often said we lost both our parents on the same day. Although we had Dad in the flesh, it was a different Dad in terms of his personality.

Once the news of my divorce and the teenage pregnancy of our friend's daughter got out in the community and our church, it caused some scandal. The church sent me a letter asking me and the girls to leave because the entire situation was difficult for them to explain to the congregation. The other family stayed at the church, and the girls' dad stayed. They thought it was best for us to leave the church.

For the first time in my life, I was without a church, home and family. At the time, it seemed like everything in my world was falling apart. My marriage, my mom died, my dad was in bad health, and my sister lived in North Carolina. I was lost and alone with two hurt and wounded little girls. It truly felt like my world seemed to be spinning out of control. The emotional pain was so heavy and unbearable that clear thinking was not at work in my life then. Every support system I thought was available was gone.

Their dad married the teenager who was pregnant with his child. They had a little girl they named Kristin. Their marriage only lasted 18 months. My daughters loved their little sister. Kristin looked so much like my older daughter, Aimee; it was unmistakable they were sisters! My girls still regularly saw their half-sister, Kristin, until one day, when Kristin was about 2, her dad gave up his rights. He signed her to be adopted by Kristin's new stepdad. At that time, my girls stopped seeing Kristin. Aimee was 11, and Melissa was nine when this happened. Their hearts and mine were broken all over again.

Spiritually, during this time, I was adrift. I had never been thrown out of anything in my life before, much less church! Thankfully, God never forsakes us or leaves us, and He certainly did not leave me then in a very dark time. The girls and I visited various churches during this time of about ten years, the strategic growth years of my daughters' lives.

Often, I would struggle with what my choices and decisions had done to my daughters' lives. Sometimes, well-meaning people would tell me I had destroyed my daughters' lives. One woman, let's just call her a church woman, said that what I had done by getting a divorce was a death sentence to my girls, sending them straight to hell. Well, let's just say I was not receiving that comment! I always had a sense inside me that I now know was and is the Holy Spirit, gently saying to me: those girls are mine, and I will lead them where I want them. Stay connected to me. Honestly, I cannot say I was in hot pursuit of God, but I was holding onto Him for dear life!

Sometime after my divorce from my first husband, I met a man on an airplane while on a business trip. We ended up getting married and were married for ten years. This second marriage required us to move to Indiana from Florida when my oldest daughter was in middle school, and my youngest was a 5th grader. This is not a great time of life for moving kids, but in keeping with my "live by the seat of my pants" decision-making style at that time, off we went.

Aimee, my oldest, counted the days she could get back to Florida and attend Florida State University. Melissa, my youngest, thrived in her new surroundings. But eventually, both girls found their footing in life. Aimee did graduate from Florida State University and later went back to college at Purdue University, Fort Wayne, and got her nursing degree. Melissa went one semester to Ball State, returned to Fort Wayne, and graduated from Purdue University, Fort Wayne, with a Communications degree. For all the poor choices I made and the unstable life the girls had to endure, God saw to it to redeem all the bad and make good from it! These girls were and are just amazing!

The girls were not the only ones to graduate college in the early 1990s; I went back to college after we moved to Fort Wayne. I graduated from Indiana Tech with a Business Management major and Psychology minor, Summa Cum Laude. It took me 14 years to complete my college, but thanks to God's grace and a lot of encouragement from my girls, it was accomplished. They were my biggest cheerleaders! I was the first one in my family to graduate from college, but my mom was not alive to see it. She would have considered it a great thing as she wanted to go to college. My dad came to my graduation but was not overly impressed as he did not hold higher education in high regard. He aspired for me to stay home and not work outside of it. Nonetheless, he was proud of me!

Not long after my college graduation, I found myself divorced again. At this time, Aimee was in college in Florida, and Melissa was finishing high school. This divorce was not near as dramatic and painful as the first one. We did not have children together, so that was certainly less emotional. We had been married ten years, though, so it was not nothing. All divorce is difficult. You certainly deal with the defeat of it all. This time, it did cause me to dig deep and look inward. I concluded at the end of this marriage that I was the common denominator in both marriages. So, I turned to the one constant I knew in my life - God!

As far as working went, I always seemed to get great jobs with good pay throughout my life. When we first moved to Fort Wayne, I worked at a hospital in the Cardio-Pulmonary Lab; then, I worked for a local HMO, where I got my health insurance license. Later, I started a small business selling group health insurance. I worked in downtown Fort Wayne in an office building that housed several small businesses. While working there, I met a man named Mike Nickols.

Chapter 4.

Mike's Conversion

As I mentioned above, taking a job at the bank had way more for me than I could have imagined. God was about to move powerfully in my life. The job at the bank was His divine steering of my life. But leading up to this time was a significant setup by God.

While in college, I was always pursuing different girls. I did this whether I had a girlfriend or not. Nothing restricted me from pursuing a relationship that I wanted. I met this girl who was a teaching assistant with whom I wanted to go out. She asked why I didn't take the class she taught, and we would see where it went. And so, I did. She taught a religion class, but not the kind of religion you think of. She was an atheist and taught us how to defend ourselves against Christianity. I also took her follow-up class as well. Debate had always been a forte of mine, and now combined with this training, I was armed and dangerous to people of faith. Trying to bring down Christians seemed to soothe the emptiness inside. I looked for and found many opportunities to tear down what I considered fairytales of people's religion.

One time in Florida on spring break, some guys from Campus Crusade were trying to witness to me. A friend of mine and I picked up the one talking and threw him in the ocean. I was not exactly a friend of Christians. It is amazing to me, looking back, how broken I was. Yet, I thought I was pretty much a gift to the world. The God I did not believe in was about to bust my chops. Having taken the path of least resistance through college, I did not see the way forward for my career. I was also in jeopardy of being drafted to the

Vietnam War as soon I graduated. The Marine Corp came to the SAE house and recruited to a special program.

Between your Junior and Senior years, you would go to officer candidate school. It was ten weeks of super boot camp. Then you went back to school, and when you graduated a year later, you could choose whether to take your officer's commission or not. You were not obligated to go into the Marine Corp. In another of my not-thought-out actions, I decided to do it. You may have heard it said that the Marines break you and then remake you. This was true in my experience. They broke me, but I would not let them remake me. I was too spoiled, self-centered, and egotistical.

After a few weeks at boot camp, I found out I had received a high number in the draft lottery, and I would not be drafted. I cannot tell you how much this little brat wanted out of my situation. I did not cooperate with the training. Due to that, I received a lot of special treatment. When I left, Mike Nickols, who could always escape anything like Houdini, was broken. My confidence in myself, wrongly placed from the start, was in shambles. What should have been a great senior year was marked by a new kind of personal doubt.

I had started dating my first wife at the end of my junior year. I was at Indiana University in Bloomington during my senior year, and she was at the extension in Fort Wayne. I was needy and broken. I limped to the end of school, and my fiancé planned the wedding.

Shortly after graduating from college in 1973, I got married and started my job. The job my dad had gotten me at the bank. Within a couple of weeks of my starting at the bank, they hired a guy who was to be a sort of partner to me. We would work together all day, every day. His name was Frank. Frank was a Christian, and he fit my stereotype of a Christian very well. By my standards, he was a square. He did not dress cool, drink, go the clubs, or cuss. He was single but did not seem to know how to appeal to women. He did not seem to pursue intellectual curiosity either. We would work together 8-10 hours every day. He would witness to me about being a Christian.

I remember thinking, I need someone or something to help me regain my mojo. To return me to the glory days of college before my senior year. This guy is a far cry from where I want to go. I would use my skill sets and training to undermine and set aside everything he said. He was not deterred, though. He would return with answers to my accusations and rebuttals in a day or two. He did this after talking with other Christians or researching on his own, and then he would bring me answers. I was curious why he did not melt and slink away under the pressure of my attacks. That was what most Christians I had met had done. I was not nice to him, but he seemed to care about me despite that. Something else, something much deeper, was going on, though.

As time went on, I began to observe something I had never entertained before. I had everything I thought was important and valuable in my value system. In that system, Frank should have been pitied for his sad situation in the hierarchy of coolness. But the hard reality was that he was actually happy. I pretended to be happy, but it was a poor imposter to what I could see in him. Something had begun to penetrate the thick armor of my soul. He had real friends. I had never had a real friend like he had. He had joy and purpose. He was comfortable in his own skin. He seemed to care more about me than anyone I had ever seen before.

Day by day, something inside me was crumbling. My confident intellectual belief system was failing just as my confidence in myself had failed a few months earlier.

One day, it was almost like I tore off my jacket representing everything I was and ran toward the life this friend told me I could access. I remember thinking I do not care about my arguments; I don't care about coolness or what all my friends would think. I wanted that joy, that peace, real friends. And whatever I must do to get into this life, I will do it. I think because of pride, I did not want Frank to help me become a Christian. Because of that, I was trying to figure it out.

One day, I "happened" to come upon a Billy Graham tract that explained salvation. I took that little pamphlet to my bedroom alone and closed the door. With excitement and trepidation, I began to read.

Billy Graham used scripture verses to explain that we are all sinners. Well, that was noticeably clear to me in my life. I could not get out of my mind all the people I had hurt and abused. Another scripture He used said that the wages of sin is death. That was explained by Billy Graham as separated from God and those we loved after we died. It also included paying a serious price for the things I had done. He also said rebellion against God poisoned opportunities for a good life here and now.

My life certainly was screaming that loud and clear. The issues of real peace, authentic joy, and significant purpose were things God was showing me were missing in my life. This was despite being able to get most of what I thought would bring me those things in the world.

Again, in the Billy Graham pamphlet, more scripture explains that the sinless Jesus Christ, who was God came to earth and chose to die in my place. Although I had fought against this and did all I could to destroy this hope for others, I knew it was true at that moment. The little booklet then gave a call to action, again using scripture. The booklet said **You must ask Jesus to forgive you of the things you have done wrong, come into your life and save you. Then bow the knee and make Him the ruler of your life.**

Standing beside my bed, I asked Jesus to forgive me and be my Savior and Lord. And then I cried. A tremendous burden was lifted off me in that moment. I felt forgiven. I was experiencing God's love and presence for the first time ever. It was like I had exited the freeway going to one destination and began a lifelong journey to the Kingdom of God. It was the summer of 1973.

One more thing I feel I should bring to your attention. Many people know that God seemed harsh and violent in the Old Testament. He killed Aaron's sons for using the wrong fire in the temple. He approved of the leaders of Israel killing thousands of people. David, a man after God's own heart, killed thousands of people. David justified killing many people according to a value system I did not understand. Hanging out with David could be extremely dangerous. Yet for those who respected God, who trusted and looked to Him, He was kind and compassionate. He protected you and guided you. He revealed His love for you.

In contrast to the God of the Old Testament, many people think that Jesus in the New Testament is all loving and forgiving. And He is if you turn to Him and become a child of God. If you put your trust in Him. If you ask Him to be your Lord and Savior. But for those that rebel against Him or look for life in places other than Him, it hasn't changed much from David's time.

Luke 19:12-15 and 27 New Living Translation

[12] He said, "A nobleman was called away to a distant empire to be crowned king and then return. [13] Before he left, he called together ten of his servants and divided among them ten pounds of silver, saying, 'Invest this for me while I am gone.' [14] But his people hated him and sent a delegation after him to say, 'We do not want him to be our king.'

[15] "After he was crowned king, he returned and called in the servants to whom he had given the money. He wanted to find out what their profits were.

After the King had rewarded those who had done well in investing, he turned to the matter of those who did not want him to be King…

[27] **And as for these enemies of mine who didn't want me to be their king—bring them in and execute them right here in front of me.'"**

For those who accept Christ, the value is beyond measure. You get adopted into God's family. You get full access to love, joy, peace, and purpose. You get to be transformed into a person of great character. You get to fellowship with God; you get the Holy Spirit as helper, all things work together for good. Your life has ultimate value and significance. And you get to live forever with Christ and all those who love Him.

When you mess up, you are treated like one of His kids. You get disciplined by a loving father who only wants good for you. However, it is a very dark future for those who think they know better than God like I did for the first 22 years of my life. God does not tolerate rebellion. If you do not know God, having accepted Christ with a true and sincere heart, fixing that needs to be your first order of business.

Chapter 5.

Beginning the Walk of Faith

I never even knew Christian music existed. Yet almost immediately after becoming a Christian, I discovered a Christian song by Nancy Honeytree, Clean before My Lord. That song impacted me deeply. It confirmed so much of what had happened. In listening to it, my experience with God in asking Him into my life was renewed and expanded. I got right into church, and all my friends and activities radically changed. I experienced "that first love" that God is after in all of us.

If you have been a Christian for long, you know that the book of our life has many chapters that do not end with "and he lived happily ever after."

Like most new believers, my life became a mixture of things. There was delight at the new peace, joy, and hope. But there was pushback from my old friends, family, and my wife. The pushback was substantial and was very threatening to my new faith. Despite that, God was looking out for me.

Having just moved to Fort Wayne from Bloomington after graduation in 1973, most of my partners in the old life were not close by. My only new friend was Frank, who I worked with and who had been sharing Christ with me for months. So, I moved into his circle of Christian friends and entered the church experience. In the same way, as it was when I played football, I took on this new life with everything that was in me. I was a changed man and had to share it with everyone, often with not the greatest diplomacy. Most of my college and high school friends soon had me in the religious nut category. And consequently, we no longer had a relationship and did not for many years.

My family resisted, but eventually, they all came to Christ. Vicki, my wife of less than six months, was initially appalled at my "conversion." This is not what she had signed up for. She had very little exposure to the process that I had gone through. She had been raised a "good Christian girl," and she felt betrayed by the whole getting saved thing.

Several months later, my wife did go forward at a citywide evangelistic event in Fort Wayne. She did it without much enthusiasm. However, she did become a Christian that day, even if it was reluctantly. Even though we were now both "Christians" on many issues, we were on quite different pages. I was a risk taker, a pioneer, charging ahead at every turn. She was a settler, risk-averse and cautious about moving forward. In my experience, her family never talked about feelings at all. You could not talk religion, politics, love, sex, or feelings with them. My family talked about everything. Often in anger at the top of our voices.

Around the time Vicki became a Christian, in 1974, there was a mission conference at the church we were going to. There was an altar call at the end of the conference to become a missionary. I was completely moved in my heart to go forward, which I did. My wife was terribly upset by the whole ordeal and refused to accept that there might be any validity to it. I thought we would be going to the mission field right away. She felt over my dead body. I said no kids now so we could go to the mission field. Somehow, we got pregnant right away.

From the get-go, I loved my new son Matt. He was the beginning of knowing the joy of having kids and see them grow into amazing people. Today, Matt, his three brothers, and Sherry's two girls are the source of some of the greatest joy in my life. Vicki and I were on quite different pages relating to intimacy and risk-taking. But we were on the same page: loving the boys and incredibly grateful for them.

For two or three years, I put missions on the back burner. But the inner calling would not go away. Three years after Matt was born, we were again in a family way, this time with twins. For several months, the increase in family size was stealing my peace. I was very upset that this increase in family size was the nail in the coffin for the mission field. When Craig and Cory, our twins, were born, God gave me a great love for them both. This was despite the fact my plans for life were being shredded.

On the church front, I was pouring myself into the ministry as a lay person. If I could not be a full-time missionary, then this must be what God had for me. Serving in any capacity should be about hearing God's direction and working hard to please Him. A significant portion of my serving was to make something of myself in this new Christian culture. And some of it was to please the church leadership that I had on a pedestal. Because the church was growing and the workers' needs were great, they were willing to use me seven days a week.

About a year after the twins were born, I began to get very discouraged in church life. It felt like appreciation had evaporated even though it seemed I was giving my whole life to the church.

I was over-committed and overworked. And I began to notice several areas that I disagreed with church leadership.

This experience of becoming disillusioned with ministry and getting hurt is so common. I have come to believe it is almost a rite of passage to the full Christian life.

Soon a flashpoint event happened. A man in the church who was a big giver had a reputation of liking little girls. It was hard to know if the rumors were true. One day at church, I came upon him and a small girl. It was not good. I did not know what to do, so I went to the pastor. He said he would take care of it, but I pressed in, saying it was illegal and something needed to be done. After a while, the pastor looked at me with real anger and said, "if you don't drop this, someone is going to be in a lot of trouble, and it won't be that guy." This sent me reeling down the road of full-blown anger and distrust that was already on.

Vicki and I decided, after seven years in the church and the only life we had known since becoming Christians, to move on. In this church, as in many, moving on was considered a breach of faith. It was never overtly stated, but in practice, you were shunned.

A couple of years before the massacre at church, I had left the banking world. This was much to the chagrin of my dad. I went into the insurance business. I was recruited away from the bank by a Christian insurance company who had been the bank's client. After a year or so with them, AFLAC recruited me away from them. Soon after, they wanted me to move to San Jose, California. Another couple we had been friends with at church who were also "hurt" and left were moving to Fresno, California. He was going to be a youth pastor. This was the icing on the cake.

The job offered, the promise of friends having gone through what we were experiencing being close by, and the pain of exiting the church made me want to go to California and "start over." It was 1980. I had been a Christian now for seven years.

As you might expect, my wife was very reluctant to leave family and move clear across the country with three young boys and no family. Especially to a place, we had never even been to. After much debate and consternation, she agreed to move.

When we got to San Jose, it was much different than I imagined. We had come to California on a wing and a prayer. We had very little money, and we had all of our possessions in the truck we had rented to move. We had looked for a place to live in California through a Christian we had met that lived there. We had agreed to lease a place via their recommendation, although we had never even seen a picture of the place.

When we arrived in California, the place we rented seemed very unsafe to my wife and me. So, we began looking for another place for a week, driving around in our U-Haul truck. We found a place that was better but not great. We finally decided to take this apartment as we saw our limited funds get eaten up by staying in hotels and eating out. My wife found a job; she was a dental hygienist. I threw myself into work. We looked for a church and tried out a few, but no place had a sense of belonging. I thought the problem was the churches, but I was really the problem. Work began replacing service in the church for the focus of my life.

AFLAC had had a very hard time making California successful for them. They had been trying various strategies for several years. One of the enticements to get me to move to California was a new program AFLAC was trying. Traditionally, regional managers recruited, trained, and sold insurance products strictly on commission and overrides. This new program would benefit me as a regional manager by providing me an office, an administrative assistant, and a budget for recruiting.

About seven months after we arrived in California, the whole AFLAC management team who was involved in the formation of this program, including my boss, were let go. That meant all the infrastructure we had built became my responsibility to fund. AFLAC "lent" me the money to continue. The new State manager was a retired drill instructor from the Marine Corps. I was sinking fast under the new expenses.

Soon, the state manager required me to move to Sacramento, where he lived and had the state office. We closed the regional office in San Jose. I was working seven days a week. Work was turning from a replacement for church to a sort of nightmare. My wife found a new job and was pretty much raising the boys by herself while I worked non-stop. And then... pregnant again. A fourth son was born in 1983. Although having additional kids seemed like a setback to my understanding of the mission God had called me to, my heart felt a great love for Tyler.

There was a hit song from a movie called Alfie. The famous line from the movie was in the song. "What's it all about Alfie? Is it just for the moment we live?" That was the question I began to ask. It was 1983. After three years of wandering, I began to seek God again earnestly. When you seek Him with all your heart, you will find Him, it says in Jeremiah.

Chapter 6.

Being Called

For six months, I fasted every Wednesday from when I got up until after church that night. Every waking moment of every day, the question seemed too always be before me... What's it all about? Who are you? Do you have a purpose?

After about six months, God began to speak to me like He had never done up to the point in my life.

That was probably the first time in my life I had sought Him with all my heart. I am not sure if it is in us of our own accord to seek God with all our heart. But He, in His mercy and grace, orchestrates events so that we are driven to seek Him. I have come to see that there is purpose in every pain, even when self-inflicted, for those who truly belong to Him.

God communicated to me in the ways He communicates with everyone. In prayer, in the Word of God, in the still small voice, through friends that love God, and through worshiping Him. He told me he had created me to do four things.

The first was to raise my children to hunger and thirst after Him.

He said to do that; you must complete a second calling that has two parts. You must keep your children in authentic corporate worship. This is so they will experience my presence. The second thing is you must keep them around authentic Christians. They must do life with the genuine article. Ones who love and know me so that they will see what the authentic Christian walk looks like.

The third thing is that you are to build your business and use it to build the Kingdom of God.

Finally, your mission field is England and Scotland. You are to look at them as if they are your children, being ever concerned about their spiritual welfare. It was like God was saying these things with a laser that burned it into my soul for days and days and days. Those callings and sense of destiny have never left me. It was the same as when I went forward at the mission conference. I thought each of these callings would begin to happen right away. When God calls us, he often takes us through a long process of preparation. This may include many trials. We can look at the life of Joseph, Moses or David, or the Apostle Paul to see how God views preparation. God's preparing me for His use has continued unabated until even now. His preparing was in ways I never suspected it could be. I could not have conceived what God was willing to do or allow to make me what he wants me to be.

Chapter 7.

Life of Struggle

Within a few months of hearing God lay out what I was called to do, I resigned from AFLAC and went on my own as an independent agent. I thought that the demands of AFLAC were too much, and I could have a more "normal" life away from them.

I had met a guy through business named Cliff. He and I formed our own agency and began to compete with AFLAC. Cliff had uniquely become a Christian. We had worked together at AFLAC for several months. One day, he called me and asked if I could come to the houseboat he and his wife Gerri lived on. I went there as he requested. We had barely sat down when he said, "Gerri and I have been hearing about this Christian life, and we want it. You seem to be a Christian. Can you help us get into this Christian life? That gave Cliff and I a special bond.

In our new agency, we were traveling all over California, trying to support our families under the difficult circumstance of starting a new business on extremely limited funds. My wife was working hard as well. She worked four days a week as a hygienist. In this season, our fourth son Tyler was born. As I mentioned above, I loved Tyler from the moment he was born. However, the additional load of another baby put more strain on Vicki and my relationship. So, with four boys, a full-time job, and a husband gone a lot, it was some difficult times, particularly for her. We went to various churches looking and struggling to find authentic worship. We struggled to make friends, let alone people that were full-on after Jesus. I thought we just could not find the right people to be friends with, but the truth was I was not the right person to be a friend. There seemed no chance to pursue missions in England or Scotland. I hoped my business would allow me to build the Kingdom of God. But I struggled to make enough to keep our heads above water. My wife, who never loved the idea of my callings, had increasing doubts. The lack of traction on many fronts resulted in our openness to change locations again.

In late 1984, we moved back to Fort Wayne. I was recruited back by Frank, my friend who had led me to the Lord and his business partner to join them in a third-party administration company that did group insurance. After a few months, the business was sold, pretty much against our will. The business needed capital investment to survive, and the company that said they would invest ended up on the day of closing, demanding they be given majority ownership as a condition of the investment. It seemed like we had no choice. So overnight, we worked for the other guy in a very corporate environment. Once again, events had turned out to be far different from my plans. Once again, it was "a gold mine in Alaska; we didn't find it there, so we moved on."

Soon, once again, change was upon us. I restarted an insurance agency for a while. I made some money, but we continued to struggle financially. Then I went back to work with Frank in a large insurance agency in Fort Wayne. The promise of great prosperity and reasonable work hours never materialized. For my wife and I, with what little time I had that was not business, our lives settled into raising the boys. I coached all my sons in baseball and basketball for ten years. This was one of the greatest times and best investment in my kids I could have ever hoped for.

As usual, life went on with a mixture of blessing and struggle. If we were focused on our sons, life was workable. But intimacy, sharing hearts, and vision for the future was a different matter. I was desperate to pursue the calling that I felt God had on me. I began another go at it by starting a church with 3 or 4 couples and with the help of a pastor I had in California. I so wanted authentic corporate worship. And I wanted fellowship with people that loved and walked with God. Nothing seemed like too big of a sacrifice to make it happen. We had a few startup meetings, hired a pastor from Texas, and opened with over 250 on the first day.

To say I was naive and inexperienced at pioneering a church would be the understatement of the year. In short, the new pastor was going in a different direction than I thought we had agreed. This led to conflict and then to my leaving. A bit later, we started another church. That church grew and prospered. I was at that church for ten years until Vicki, and I got a divorce. Both of those churches are flourishing to this day. Yet, neither one gave me the sense that I was accomplishing what God had told me I must do for the kids.

As time went on, I became more and more frustrated. Finally, in 1988 I got to go to England for the first time. As we flew over the coast of England, I felt an incredible sense of destiny and anticipation. To me, I had arrived in the promise land. To my wife, Vicki, we had descended into hell. Every place we visited, I was envisioning building a future there. I loved every town, every church, every person we met. The more I talked about living and ministering there, the more my wife felt that I did not have her interest at heart, which was true. At one point, she tried to jump out of the moving car to start back to America. She wanted out because the discussion about Great Britain was so uncomfortable and threatening. When we returned to States, I was all about wanting to make ministry in England happen.

She felt the moving, starting churches, running my own business was not working. It made her question whether I had heard from God at all. Scotland and England were the cherry on top of her view that this was not what she wanted. Her position was, I needed to give up my business and work for the other guy. As a family, we needed to accept the worship and group of people around us as our friends and the ones to do life with.

And most importantly, quit indulging in the pipe dream of being a missionary in Scotland and England. As I mentioned above, it did work out for me to be "working for the other guy," and we did not change churches or our circle of relationships. I had a great relationship with each of my sons. Yet, I was haunted by the sense of not fulfilling what I believed God had told me to do. There seemed to be no way to change the situation. It was like Groundhog Day!

As I have described, in my high school and college days, I worked hard at developing skills at a very worldly lifestyle. It was at the core of who the natural man was in me. When I accepted Christ, I was given a new nature that loved God and wanted to live for Him, but the old nature lies in wait. I began to doubt God's plan because this was way off what I thought it would be. I was questioning if He had my best interest at heart. My need to fulfill what I understood to be the calling on my life just could not seem to get traction.

When we begin to doubt His ability to control what happens to us and its outcome, the old man is energized and rises up.

Three times in the last years of our twenty-three-year marriage, I had gotten into a sort of "office wife" situation. An office wife is someone who you have a connection with at work, church, or anywhere where a ongoing close relationship is built. Someone with whom you typically share responsibilities and accomplish things together during business or other activity. But the trust in the person and the sharing experiences develops a relationship that is more personal than with other people in the work environment. For me, it was some sort of pain control to have a "friend" at work or church that I could confide in. It was like a drug that I ran to for relief. Each time I shared a connection in areas of emotional and life support that were inappropriate. When this happens, most people, in hindsight, asks themselves some questions. What was I thinking? What caused me to do that? Where can I place the blame other than on myself? How do I get out of this? And after a while, what am I going to do?

So, what was I thinking? There is a song by Waylon Jennings, "Looking for Love in All the Wrong Places." I am sure that was part of it. But for me, it was more. It was looking for affirmation in all the wrong places. Looking for hope in all the wrong places. Looking to hide from myself the reality of where I was. It was finding pain relief in all the wrong places.

Each time, when a "friendship" with another woman broke into a real, acknowledged relationship, I ended it within a week or so. I do not think that was meritorious on my part. It was some part fear of God, some part fear of people, and some concern for my family, especially my sons. While it did not meet my definition of physical adultery, it was adultery, nonetheless. Each time, it was wrong and a great personal failure for me. I am sure it happened because of my emotional loneliness and unmet needs. But it also was a lack of character and fruit of the Spirit in my life.

I began to see something I was completely blind to for many years. Although I was sure I was pursuing God's plan for my life, my flesh was leading. Not God's Spirit. Besides the fact that there was no fruit in pursuing my calling, I was wounding and hurting many people. This happened because I was not trusting God and waiting for Him to move. In my self-focused pursuit of what I thought was right, I was doing it in my own strength. This was far more a work of the flesh than God's Spirit.

As you can imagine, finding emotional support in other women did not improve the trust and confidence of my wife toward me. My personal failings created many new obstacles in our life. It made the reconciliation of the very different ways we saw life and the future even more difficult. In my mind, I had been trying to live for God for 23 years, and both of us were extremely disappointed in the fruit.

In this atmosphere at home, the business I was working for at this time had a split between the owners. Out of that split, I was offered to form a business with two partners from the original firm. My wife was dead set against it. She had settled on the fact that for her to feel right about the way forward, I needed to work for the other guy. In other words, work for a company as a salaried employee and not owning the business.

Nevertheless, I plowed ahead. Now I was back in the world of owning my own business. I also was still very much frustrated with our experience in corporate worship. While we had "friends," from my view, there was no one with whom I felt that deep comradery of a real friend. Now I can see that the problem with having the kind of friends I wanted was not with them. It was with me. Also, I felt responsible for the spiritual condition in England and Scotland, but there was no fruit. This also drove a deeper and deeper wedge between us. I threw myself into the new business, worked long hours, and that became that focus of my life. Our marriage relationship was way off the page now in many areas. Areas that are common when the relationship is deteriorating. These festered behind the scenes.

I was very committed to the concept of marriage and not getting a divorce, so I saw no way forward. At some point, it was clear we were coming apart. So, we started going for counseling. After a while, we were meeting with three different counselors at the same time. The final break came for me when my wife gave me the ultimatum. She was supported in this by one of the counselors. She felt that if our marriage was to go forward, I would have to agree to five things first, that I would give up trying to find some elusive kind worship that was not present in our church. She felt what I was looking for didn't even exist. The second qualification was that I would accept our social life and group of friends. There would be no more pining for a bond of friendship around an understanding of God and ministry. The third qualification was I would have to give up the business. I needed to get a job working for a salary as an employee. The fourth qualification was she would set the level of intimacy between us, and I would accept it without argument. The idea was, what I was looking for in a marriage relationship was another fantasy. The fifth qualification was that I would give up the idea of having any ministry in England and Scotland.

Now I do not blame her for anything today. And even then, I understood her position. All five qualifications she was demanding, I had been trying and failing at for 23 years. My thinking at that time was that she was asking me to set aside everything God asked me to do. I could not do it. The marriage was over for me on that day. Yet I could not even say the word divorce, let alone hire an attorney and file for one. I had resolved that I would have two lives. One that was "family life" with her and then my business and the life that came out of those relationships. This created great conflict within me on several levels.

Even though I was accepting moving into a new sort of dual life, it seemed like another big failure. There was no way to reconcile my faith and where my life was at. Sherry, my wife today of 25 years, was one of my partners in the business. Sherry and I did not have an acknowledged relationship. Yet, in looking back from the distance of time, I was happy and glad to have her supportive relationship in business. And it provided some safety net for my personal trials.

At some point, my wife filed for a separation of some kind, forcing me to leave the house and get my own place. My attorney said the way the separation was filed, it was really a filing for divorce. Anyway, in 1996, that is where it ended up, a filing for divorce. Our divorce was final in 1997. In short order, Sherry and I did have a relationship, and before long got married. We did not do it right. We were in the wrong from the get-go. We did not wait; we did not get much counsel; we forged ahead. Our relationship did not cause the divorce, but it made the way forward in going through with it a lot easier.

It should have been a disaster. Most people I knew said it would be. Deep inside, I was very afraid it would be myself, but it was not. Somehow, we have had the most amazing marriage anyone could hope for.

Chapter 8.

God Redeems My Failures

Looking back on it now, a few things happened that impacted how the marriage between Sherry and I turned out.

First, divorce is an undeniable cataclysmic failure, especially for an outspoken Christian. Some sins we can hide. This one is very public and cannot be hidden. It encompasses almost every area of life. And there are always plenty of people who are there to remind you that you have had a fatal failure. In this situation, you are forced to face the fact of your failure. When in desperation, if you turn fully to God, He redeems the most horrible situations.

Secondly, I did know God, and I did want to please Him and to become what He wanted me to be. In my own flawed way, I had been asking for His help all along the path. So, through no merit of my own, I decided to take the way of admitting my failure. And asking God daily for help and direction. He was very gracious in giving it to me.

Andy Stanley, the pastor of Northpoint ministries, says when failure occurs in our life, we all have a story that we tell. It is full of spin. It is about how whatever we have not succeeded at is not our fault. And to a large extent, it is not our fault. It is just not the whole story.

No matter how much we justify what happened in every failure, especially in the failure of a marriage, we all have skin in the game. I knew the scripture enough to know I violated the rules. And no matter how I looked at it, I was the captain of the ship that sank.

The other night, a new Christian guy was talking at a men's meeting. He went on and on with his argument that what had happened to him was unjust and he was a victim. Watching him, God reminded me of times in my own life where I was busy justifying my behavior. It dawned on me that if I could convince a million people that my story was correct, it would not make me feel whole. This is because deep inside, I knew I had skin and blame in the game. I had spent many years justifying why I was where I was and why the supposed callings on my life were not happening. So, I knew that going the way of justifying my behavior would not bring life to me. So, I decided I would give over to God the ownership of what I thought were my callings. I gave Him the right to direct my path, not just advise me while I reserved the final decisions for myself.

The third thing was I believed in the callings God had said were on my life. That made me determined to stay in my kid's life when many wanted me out.

As many of you have experienced, the woman usually gets the kids in a divorce. She is no longer a friend of the man she was married to. Often, she starts a new life where she does not want the man to be a part of it. She often rallies friends and family to push the man away because of being hurt and wounded. Whether at sporting events, education events, or family events, it is very easy to feel unwanted and to just fade away. Again, God helped me make some decisions here that were very significant in shaping my future. Somewhere in here, God gave me the conviction that I would pay every dime of my child's support on time. By His grace, I never missed a week. I also decided to keep my kids in Christian schools and Christian college. And pay for my portion of it beyond my support. This meant I was giving to Vicki and the kids more than I made for an extended period. But God provided. Finally, I decided that no matter who tried to stop me, I would be in my kid's life. I would love them and try to work through this negative impact on their lives with God by my side.

At first, two of my sons did well with it, and two struggled with me. Sherry and I decided that we would be there for them even when they did not want us. At the time Sherry and I were married, our two oldest, my son and her daughter, were in college. Her youngest daughter and my three other sons were in high school. We attended every one of their high school basketball games. And once these two were in college, we visited them regularly. We went where they were on summer mission trips, even though sometimes they did not want us to be there. We tried to say we loved them in every way we could.

Over time, healing began to come. There were many exceedingly difficult times of rejection, hurt, and shame. One time at the twins' basketball game at their Christian school, Sherry and I went to the game alone. Usually, we went with other friends or family. When we sat down, everyone around us got up and moved. This left us sitting in the middle of a section with empty seats all around by ourselves.

My relationship with Aimee and Melissa, Sherry's daughters, was an oasis for me at that time. They both took me in as a bonus, Dad in the most awesome ways. My relationship with them has never floundered. Both of the girls worked for us in the business and really were daughters to me in the most significant ways.

Navigating divorce with any measure of success is not for the faint of heart. All the boys have had times of anger and rejection of Sherry and me. But we kept believing that God was with us. And we knew He wanted us to persevere. Through that, sweet reconciliation and ever-increasing healing did flow. Our sons have all, at times, rejected Sherry and then restored the relationship.

Navigating bonus moms and dads and bonus brothers and sisters is incredibly challenging. It takes putting God's interest and, really, God's interest in those we are incredibly angry with ahead of our own interest.

Every one of us eventually made real progress at it, despite the adversity. This is because we all knew God and wanted to be pleasing in His sight. For the last 15 years, with occasional bumps, we have had extraordinarily strong, loving, and involved lives between Sherry and I, all six of our kids, and our 13 grandkids. All six of the kids, their spouses, and all the grandkids are today the best of friends. It could not have happened without supernatural help.

God helped us to put knowing Him, receiving His healing. And fulfilling our destiny ahead of the pain that personal failure produced. Every one of our kids had to find their own personal faith. They had to endure being hurt and the unfair, unjust things that happened to them. Each of them had to face difficult choices repeatedly. Will I forgive? Will I keep believing in God's goodness? Can I still believe that He has a plan for me? Can I trust that He loves me? They had to reject self-pity. They had to have mercy on Sherry and me and many others. They had to decide they believed what God says.

Each of them has had many years of making many good decisions and asking for forgiveness for themselves and for others. Out of that has come deep relationship with God that is their own. It has also produced fruitful service to the Kingdom in each of their lives. They have all become oak trees in the Kingdom of God. Most people say they want their kids to do better than they did. That usually means financial prosperity. Our kids have all exceeded us in financial accomplishment. Yet that pales in comparison to the value of their spiritual accomplishment, their intimacy with God. Their being transformed into Christ's likeness. And their finding and fulfilling their personal destinies. God is good, and He delivers what He promises.

The best thing is they all love and care for each other. Sherry and I have been married for twenty-five years. There have been many ups and downs with all the family relationships. But today, I would not trade the way it has turned out for anything. Adversity, of all stripes, given to God will make awesome fruit.

From my perspective, Sherry and I had the usual marriage adjustments. Considering the adversity of our world, it should have destroyed us, yet it seemed to bond us together. Shortly after we were married, she told the Lord she had been running her life and wanted Him to take over. Immediately, Joyce Meyer's teachings came into her life. She started reading and watching Christian programs day and night. Often, for several years, she would only sleep maybe two or three hours. She began to know God more deeply than she ever had before. God gave her a strong hunger to understand about Him and His ways. She read many books by Billy Graham, Charles Stanley, Joyce Meyer, and many others. We were buying new bookcases to accommodate all the books. My desire for the things of God had very quickly become our desire.

Sherry was very much on the same page as I was. We both were full-on after knowing God, being internally healed, and bearing fruit. We both wanted to be all that God created us to be and to serve Him with all that was in us. For Sherry's life, the turning point was the day she decided to let God take over her decision-making. She decided that she was the common denominator in the failures of her life. Abundant life began to happen. This was true for both of us. There is no doubt that Sherry's giving herself to God was crucial. If not, she would have been destroyed by the adversity of divorce and remarriage. Every day she got more committed to loving all the boys and their sisters, no matter what happened.

Another thing that changed almost immediately was our business began to flourish. It had been on life support up until then. As it began to thrive, lots of rewards came our way. In the insurance business, we were in, when you do well, there were often trips that you win. We have seen a great deal of the world because of that. And we were often able to include the kids. Although they did not always appreciate it at the time, it bonded us and gave us a common experience. This has served our relationships very well.

We were having success with our business. And we were moving forward in restoring the love and fellowship of our family. We were active in church. But we still had no sense of fulfillment in worship. We had no ministry cause to believe in that we were a part of. And other than family, no one we considered to be hungering and thirsting after God to do life with. It is easy to question what you believe you have heard from God. Does what I have heard have validity when so long of a time passes without more fruit? But in this case, I could not get loose from what God had said to me all those years ago. Still, the kids and the business were positive advances on my perception of my calling. But making a real difference in people other than family was as elusive for us as it always had been for me.

There was one remarkably interesting thing that happened before my heart attacks. What seemed a very insignificant thing that just dropped into our lives set up our future. As is often the case, I had no idea what was happening. As Sherry said, she was being immersed in scripture and theology. She had many teachers, but the most significant one was Joyce Meyer.

One day, Sherry was going to the Christian bookstore to get one of Joyce's new books, and I went along. I was browsing through the store. I came upon a VHS tape on worship. There was a lady worship leader on the front from Hillsong, Australia, who seemed so full of energy that I was intrigued. After looking it over, I told Sherry I would get this tape. She was fine with it, and off we went.

When we got home, our son Tyler, who was a senior in high school at the time, was there, and the three of us decided to watch the tape. It was Darlene Zschech and Hillsong Worship. We were completely mesmerized. After an hour or so, we were all crying. I was overcome with emotion. I kept saying, this is it; this is the worship God has been telling me about for over 20 years. There was such a powerful witness in my soul that this was the worship I was to have in my life and my family's life. It was like I had discovered the throne room of God.

At the end of the tape, it had an advertisement for Hillsong Leadership College. Tyler said, "I want to go there to school." And within a month after graduating high school, he was off at 18 years old to Australia. No one in the family had ever been to Australia. It was a true moment of trusting God for all of us. In a truly short time, Hillsong, Darlene, and her husband Mark would be significant people in our lives and a big part of what precipitated this book.

I have noticed something in a new way in scripture. Many people were called to do something at an early age. Abraham, Moses, Joseph, David, the Apostle Paul, and many others were examples of this. They were called. Then they experienced constant failure for an extended time. They had various kinds of wilderness experiences. This was because they tried to do it in their own strength, as we all often do. God was making them into the people who could do what He asked. They learned humility and to trust fully in God. Then the calling began to happen because God brought it to pass.

Sherry and I were cruising along with life. Life was getting better and better. It seemed good and normal. Then I had three heart attacks, and the world changed.

I will continue shortly, but first, we want you to catch up on Sherry's end of the story.

Chapter 9.

Sherry's Story of God's Mercy

On April 10, 1997, Mike and I married. Now I am on my third marriage. Mike's mom passed away the day after we married. This, in some odd way, connected me to his family. She was in the hospital and hospice for a month. Before her death, we stayed by her side the entire time. After his mom's funeral, my dad, who lived in Florida, wanted to come see us. At the same time, we were moving into our new home.

Together, Mike and I, at the start of our marriage, had six kids from age 13 to 21. Right away, two of those kids wanted to bring a girlfriend and a boyfriend to live with us over the summer between college classes. My dad came to stay for what ended up being three months. We all moved into to our new house at the same time. Now, this should have been an unmitigated disaster in the natural. But I made a monumental decision on May 3, 1997. God moved supernaturally in our lives from that moment to this.

While sitting on our new couch in our new home filled with lots of people, I sat down to have my morning coffee. This was like every other day at that time in my life. Suddenly, it hit me! Here I am married three times. I have two kids of my own, four stepsons, and my dad living here. I absolutely do NOT want this marriage to end! What went wrong in my life? I realized the common denominator in all this was me! I had been making decisions over my life. Decisions that impacted my daughters. And here we were, where I never thought I would be in my early 40s and on my third marriage.

I decided in that moment to give up control of daily life decisions and to trust God to do whatever He thought best for me. I knew it would require change and letting go of old ways. I came up with this saying: **People don't change until the pain of staying the same is greater than the pain of change.** That was me at that moment.

On that day, a decision was made. From that moment forward, God would make the calls over my life. As Mike mentioned, that was the day God led me to Joyce Meyer. That day began a lifelong journey of knowing God. No longer knowing about God but knowing Him personally. God was teaching me exactly what I asked for: daily direction.

Looking back on it now, it is easy to see my early Christian life was lived through the church. So, when that connection got severed, so did my direction. I took it upon myself to make the calls. Our lives are not meant to live alone; we are created relationally and to abide with our Father who created us. He is always calling us to Him. Most of the time, we do not hear it because of the all the static we have in our lives. He is faithful even when we are not.

One day, I came across some of my old journals from more than 20 years ago. As I was reading them, I thought, who is this person? Did I write that? God put that in my hands to show me how much I had changed. He was saying; you can trust me the rest of the way. What He used to bring that change in me was certainly not what I thought it would be. It never is the way we think it will be!

Mike and I love to travel. We think it is not only fun but educational and very spiritual. One thing for sure about life with Mike — it is an ADVENTURE!

Adventure is not so much what I am looking for. But I can tell you that God loves adventure. He is happy to use it for teaching His children about Him!

Here we were, married, with six children between us, a new home, a thriving business, and a contented spiritual life. Yet, we were about to take off on another big adventure. This one, though, not only would change our lives but would be etched in eternity. And it would bring change in many other people's lives as well.

Chapter 10.

The Setup to a Journey to the Other Side-Mike

Weddings are one of the greatest times we enjoy. They are a place where you experience some of best things in life. Weddings are full of joy and laughter. There is the sense of expectation in the air. The dancing, the music, and the food add a special atmosphere. And then you have the renewal of relationships gone dormant by time and distance. There is an air of excitement when planning a wedding. Most people do their best to augment the mood with natural and manmade beauty. This includes beautiful churches, flowers, awesome architecture, beaches, and mountains. Many times, it is the best that is available wherever the union is to take place.

Our daughter, Melissa, decided she wanted to have a "destination" wedding in Florida, where she was born. It was a winter wedding, and Indiana is not the place in January for an outdoor celebration. Her biological dad, Sherry's first husband, lives in Orlando, Florida. So, Missy decided to have the wedding in Florida, not in Orlando but on the beach in South Florida.

It was a beautiful wedding in the city of Bal Harbor. All the family was there, and it was a great and Christ-centered day. Our family loves cruises, and we love celebrating life together. Sherry's daughter and my bonus daughter, Melissa, decided that after the wedding, the family should go on a cruise to celebrate her wedding. And celebrate we did. Twenty of us were together on the cruise, snorkeling, body surfing, and zip lining. We also went to shows and saw the sights in the various ports.

On the next to the last night of the cruise, we moored at an industrial port outside of Playa del Carmen, Mexico. My wife, Sherry, and I and our son Tyler were out late in the day in a jeep we had rented. We had driven up to Cancun to see the resorts and do some bodysurfing. It was an awesome day. We got back to the ship late and missed dinner in the dining room. Missing dinner was no problem on the ship as there are many awesome dinner venues 24 hours a day. We went up to the top of ship to the buffet to have dinner.

As usual on a cruise ship, the food was excellent, and we were having great fellowship with each other. I suddenly had what felt like extreme heartburn. Unbeknownst to me, I had been having angina that I thought was heartburn for some time.

I was sitting in the middle seat at a table for eight, and there was a table full of people behind me. I did not have any antacid, so I said let me out; I am going to get some ice cream to see if that will quiet down this burn. I stood up, took a step, and collapsed. The pain escalated to an almost unbearable level. Or so I thought at the time. I later found out it can be much worse. The action then got fast and furious around me. Sherry started yelling out, is there a doctor here? Someone had dialed 911.

Since we did not have working cell phones, Tyler ran to a computer with internet and emailed a request for prayer to his friends and mentors at Hillsong Leadership College in Sydney, Australia, where he lived. He also emailed a request to pray to our church back in Indiana. Both places had extensive prayer teams. So, within a minute, people were praying for me all around the world.

A group of African American ladies was in the dining room with us. They were all part of a missionary society. They rushed over and laid hands on me, and started praying.

A doctor came up to Sherry and said, in a strong Spanish accent, *I am a doctor. May I help?* Sherry said to her, "please help." The ship's emergency response team arrived in short order. They began to take me to the emergency facility on the ship. As I was being wheeled on a gurney to the emergency facility, the pain would spike up and then come down. I kept shouting, "it's coming back! It's coming back!"

In the emergency room, the pain was down, but my blood pressure was 250 over 150. My EKG was going crazy. A disagreement erupted between the charge nurse and the doctor helping me. This created a sense of complete chaos for me. That chaos would soon pale in comparison to what happened next.

The ship's doctor told us the condition of my heart was unstable, so we could not stay on the ship. They were not sure what was wrong with my heart, but they knew it was not good.

Tomorrow was a day at sea, and they could not take care of me. The ship was already leaving late, and I had to get off within 15 minutes. I could take one person with me.

It was midnight in a rural industrial area of Mexico. I did not have mental clarity due to drugs, the pain, and the confusion. Sherry nor I spoke Spanish. We were leaving a party of 20 people, including our kids, behind with no means of communication.

At that time, cell phones did not work on ships or in Mexico. Rory Siren, our son-in-law, had $200 cash in his pocket that he gave to Sherry, or she would have had no cash. As we left the ship, an ambulance was waiting. We got in the ambulance and departed to we did not know where. My blood pressure in the ambulance was still 250 over 150. The Mexican EMT's were very concerned, but Sherry had no idea what they were saying. They were trying to figure out where to take me.

It turned out to be Playa del Carmen. They had a "hospital" there. It had a dirt floor. Bicycles were in the entry that belonged to the staff. Everything else was concrete, including the beds. I was put in a room with a single light bulb hanging from the ceiling. The bed was iron and had a crank like the beds from World War II. There was an EKG machine that looked like it had come from Radio Shack. I was pretty much out of it from whatever drugs they had given me.

All these issues left Sherry in an unbelievable position. Imagine being in a country that does not speak your language. You are in the worst medical facility you have ever been in your life. Your husband is pretty much unconscious. You cannot communicate with anyone around you. The nurse had a single syringe that she used on all patients and put it back in her pocket. The IV was a large glass unlabeled bottle. The hospital provided no food or drink for me, let alone Sherry. The only place for Sherry to sleep was on a concrete slab they called a bed. The on-call doctor was a pediatrician who arrived on a bicycle. Somehow, we survived until morning. Everything had to be paid in full, in cash, or credit card immediately.

Around noon, I was feeling better. The pain had stopped, and my vitals had stabilized. Even though the facilities were primitive, the care I received was excellent. They said they had done all they could for me, and I had to be transferred to the Cancun hospital and a cardiologist.

Chapter 11.

Out of Mexico - Mike's View

We exited the taxi in front of the hospital. There was no emergency entrance. We found ourselves in a small waiting room, sort of like a 1950s doctor's office.

At first, we were alone in the room. There was a receptionist's desk, but the receptionist was not there when we arrived. She hardly was ever there. After a while, some other Americans came into the waiting room. They were a 50ish couple on vacation when their son collapsed in the ocean while body surfing. They had brought him to the hospital unconscious. The family was not allowed to be back with him, so they waited in the room we were in.

The parents of this young man did not speak Spanish. And the occasional receptionist did not speak English. So, this family was in the dark, similarly to how Sherry had been the night before. They were desperate to get their son back to Houston. I am sure they had much higher confidence in the medical teams in the US. They feared the worst from what surely seemed a lower level of treatment. The inability to communicate in Mexico made it worse.

As we mentioned already, Sherry and I have sold health insurance for forty years. We have sold travel medical coverage for over 20 years. On all our trips worldwide, we always purchased the coverage for medical, evacuation, and other help when out of the country. Somehow in the hustle bustle of the wedding planning, we overlooked purchasing the coverage this time. The one time we really needed it! Still, we knew that if they had International Medical Insurance, it would help these people get their son back to Houston. Sherry asked them, and it turned out they did have the coverage. Sherry helped them connect to IMG, and soon they were on their way to Houston. Unfortunately, we never heard the outcome for their son. Nevertheless, it was a God moment. We prayed together with them; we were able to make a small contribution to help them. This is how God operates if we want Him to use us. In the chaos of our own situation, he opens windows to be of use.

We were in this waiting room for several hours. We would ask the receptionist what was up — when we were going to see somebody. She would always repeat "dos minutos" (two minutes) which became a saying of ours for years to come.

We also observed another interesting phenomenon. The doctors would stand in a circle outside the hospital, smoking cigarettes. They did it where everyone could see them. As time marched on, we were getting more and more uneasy. We noticed it was starting to get dark, and we had no plan for when we left the hospital.

Sherry and I discussed it, and she went to the pay phone in front of the hospital. This was right where the doctors were smoking. She called American Airlines, the airline we had flown on to Florida for the cruise. They told her there were no flights back to the US from Cancun that night. Tomorrow we could get a flight, but the cost was $1,350 a ticket. Sherry would not give up and kept them talking. Finally, they told her there was only one flight back to South Florida that night. It was departing at 6:30 on Iberia Air. He also told her no seats were available; they had oversold the flight. It was already 5:45, and we had not seen the doctor yet.

Getting a flight out that night was not looking good. Shortly after, they called us to come back and see the doctor. It was a lady cardiologist. She was genuinely nice and did speak English but with a very strong Mexican accent. She examined me, did an EKG, and ran some blood test, and then after a while, came back in to discuss the situation.

She said, "Well... these tests say you did not have a real heart attack, but my intuition says something bad is going on. I am going to release you, but I want you to get out of my country as soon as possible, and until you do, drink two "alcoholies" a day." She meant it. I was to have two alcoholic drinks every day until we were out of Mexico. And with that, she dismissed us. It was 7 pm. It is now dark, and we are in a Mexican city we have never been in before. Who knows if I am going to have another incident? However, we know our God and His absolute faithfulness over the years. We prayed and decided to take a taxi to the airport.

Our thinking was, sometimes there is another flight that the major airlines do not know about. We figured there would be lots of hotels around the airport if we had to stay over. The chances seemed extremely high we would have to stay overnight. It turned out the drive to airport was about 45 minutes from the hospital. After driving for about 30 minutes, we started trying to communicate with the taxi driver. We asked him where a good place to stay around the airport would be. Through much trying and signaling, he informed us that there were no hotels near the Cancun airport. The closest place to get a hotel was near the hospital, but if we wanted a hotel we would be comfortable in, we would have to go back to the resort area.

Our hearts sank. It was going to be extremely late in a place we did not know good areas from bad. We would have to try to find a hotel in January. This is high season in Cancun. We found ourselves in even more desperate prayer than we had been already. We needed guidance and protection, and wisdom. At this point, we felt like, "Oh my gosh, this does not look good!" But as is always the case, God had a plan.

When we arrived at the airport, we saw a sign saying the flight to Ft. Lauderdale on Iberia had been delayed. It was now scheduled for 9 pm. We ran inside the terminal at 8:15. We still had the problem of "overbooked" to face, but we ran to the Iberia ticket desk. No one was there. We knocked, found a bell to ring, and yelled, but no one came. I could hear someone talking in the back, so I jumped the counter and returned to where they were. Four people were laughing and talking away. When they heard me come in the room, you can imagine the look as they turned to see who this intruder was. One of them spoke English, and I said we were desperate to get back to Florida tonight and needed their help.

She began typing on a computer and said we have two seats left. I said we will take them, not even asking the cost. Within 30 minutes, we were on our way to Florida. And the tickets were only $318 each. Now that seemed like a miracle to us! But in the tapestry of life, God has been faithful like this to us a thousand times. This incident is almost a metaphor for life. You start off, it looks bad, it gets worse. It seems impossible; then, God comes through in ways you never even dreamed of. One of the great advantages of doing life as a child of God.

Once we landed in Ft. Lauderdale, we needed a hotel. We did not have any hotel that we knew to call. The Holiday Inn jingle with their phone number kept coming to mind, so we called them. They had a room, and they picked us up at the airport. What a country! The next morning, we went back to the Ft. Lauderdale airport that we had originally flown into for the cruises. Low and behold! All the kids were there, having returned from the ship after the cruise ended! Mind you; we had no communications with them all the entire time we were in Mexico or after returning to Fort Lauderdale! The kids had no idea where we were or what had happened to us. We were amazed at how good God was to put all of this together with perfect timing. Reunion time and back to Indiana. We thought, wow, what an adventure! We also thought it is over. But it was yet to begin.

Chapter 12.

Mexico Through Sherry's View

Sometimes, a little knowledge can be a detriment, not an asset. I have a medical background. As already mentioned, I worked in a cardio lab at a hospital, so was somewhat familiar with EKG's.

So, it was easy to see Mike's EKG was not looking good. The ship's doctor was Greek. He was adamant that Mike needed to get off the ship. The ship nurse was a UK citizen (sounded like she was English). Both of them had no bedside manners, so there was no encouragement or direction from them on what was ahead for us.

The ship gave us 15 minutes to gather some things and disembark the ship. We exited from the ship's bowels, where cargo comes on and off. My daughters helped me think of the most important things to take with us. We could not know how long we would be there or what was ahead. We selected some clothes, medicines, toiletries, a large bottle of water (this would be all Mike and I had to eat or drink for two days), and my Bible! Off we went around midnight (after holding up the ship's departure for a while).

A Mexican ambulance with Spanish-speaking EMTs was flashing its bright lights on the shore and the ship. Our children standing there in the door where cargo would go in, looking terrible forlorn. This was Melissa's honeymoon. It was supposed to be a joyous time. A time for family to come together and celebrate. And here we were, leaving them in a situation that was far from joyous or celebratory. My heart sank as I was helpless to do anything for them or Mike. I simply had to trust God.

The EMTs placed Mike in the back of the ambulance. They motioned for me to ride up front with the driver, who, by the look on his face, looked like it was his first ride! Meanwhile, in the back of the ambulance, they were working on Mike intensely. They were speaking in Spanish so fast, making the drama worse. I could see the numbers on the blood pressure reading, and it was getting worse — 262/188! Wow! Stroke, heart attack, death!? My mind was racing. Later, we discovered a disagreement over what hospital to take Mike to. One thought Cancun (a 45-minute drive), and one thought Playa del Carmen, which was only about 10 minutes away. Playa del Carmen was much closer so Playa del Carmen it was.

Welcome to the Hotel California of hospitals, although I must tell you the loving care from these sweet people who were doing their very best under most difficult surroundings was helpful.

The hospital had dirt floors in the lobby. It had rough cement walkways and stairs, and upstairs they even had hospital beds that were rough cement. The ER was a room with a bare light bulb dangling from an electrical cord. The bed was a World War II vintage metal bed with a crank on the end. My chair was a plastic patio chair. The doctor was a woman pediatrician. She was loving and kind and took this very seriously.

Currently, there was no nurse, but one would come later during daytime hours. The doctor did it all. The EMTs had already put in the IV lines. The doctor brought a glass bottle of an unlabeled liquid to inject into Mike. Whatever it was, it calmed him down and brought his blood pressure readings down. She was a special caregiver. Doctor Love, I decided to call her. She brought what looked like a Radio Shack-type EKG machine and hooked Mike up for regular readings. Although I am no doctor, the readings did seem to get more stable.

Finally, Mike was asleep. It was me and Doctor Love and the eerie walls of this cement hospital. This was combined with some noise from the streets of Playa del Carmen. No one communicated with words because I spoke no Spanish, and Dr. Love spoke no English. She did show me to a room upstairs.

Every room upstairs was empty. This room had a bed made of cement and a rudimentary toilet that worked! I sat on the hard, cold bed and cried. Then a feeling of guilt for being weak came over me, and I opened my Bible to Psalms and began reading. I so love the Psalms. I identify with David, who wrote much of it. He was such an emotional person, crying out one moment, then declaring his faith in God the next, and on to being a warrior. This is so my personality! I could not sleep, so I went downstairs and pulled my little plastic chair over to Mike's bedside. I put my hand on his chest to feel his heart beating and fell asleep.

About 3:00 a.m., a young man came into the hospital, changing the calm atmosphere. He was very loud and had been in a fight. He was very intoxicated. There was no security in this place, so once again, Dr. Love handled the entire thing.

She stitched up this rowdy guy and sent him on his way. My personality also has a real bent toward security. So, this was a bit unsettling. But thanks to our sweet and amazing doctor, all was well. Mike was sleeping through the entire ordeal. His readings continue to show some unusual activity, but nothing like what was happening while on the ship.

Sometime around 7:00 a.m., all hell broke loose. A Mexican tour bus had an accident. An American woman on the bus had her hip and pelvis crushed. It was a true medical crisis. There were some other more minor injuries, and those could wait. Great news, though, this hospital had an orthopedic doctor they sent for.

By this time, a sweet, young nurse came to work. She had white stockings, a white three-corner hat, and an all-white uniform. She rode in on her bicycle. Another person rode their bicycle into the hospital and laid it on the dirt floor. She was the phlebotomist! So, the phlebotomist drew some blood from Mike. She also drew some from the woman with the hip/pelvic injury, and then she summoned the orthopedic doctor!

I thought this was a dream or nightmare. I was not sure which. But Dr. Love's loving sense and commanding presence kept me from a complete breakdown. (I am 100% convinced she was an angel sent by God).

I began asking God to send me someone. Someone who spoke English. And could give me some information, comfort, and encouragement. I needed it. The husband and children of the injured woman on the bus needed comfort, too, so I went to encourage them.

As Mike mentioned, we sold travel insurance for over 20 years. When I was with these people, I asked the man if they had by chance bought an international travel policy. He said they did, so I told him to call them immediately, and they will coordinate her care and take care of them. He did that, and it was not long until they came for her and flew her to Miami for surgery. Still, it was a few hours of primal screaming from the pain of a broken hip and crushed pelvis. She had no pain killers other than Tylenol. This was enough to send her family and me over the top toward going crazy!

When the lady and her family left the hospital, someone came and got me. They said in Spanish, *you have a phone call.* I could understand "telefono"! So, I went to the phone thinking, who in the world is calling as no one knew where we went. I say hello, and on the other end is our then daughter-in-law, Jena. She was not allowed to go on the cruise because she had recently given birth to our grandson, Micah, and he was too young to cruise. The fact that she was on the line was astonishing!

When I heard Jena's voice speaking in English, babble came from my mouth. *How did you find me? Have you heard from the other kids? Mike is still alive. I am half crazy. We do not know what is going on and have no clue what they will do. Mike is calm and comfortable. I have bottled water that my daughter's husband gave me when I left the ship, but the hospital has no food. Who cares about food?*

Finally, I took a breath and let her explain how she located me by telephone. She called every hospital in that area of Mexico looking for us and found us! She spoke some Spanish, and that helped. After she called, the hospital got an interpreter to come over and communicate with me. She promised to try to pass on this information to our kids and friends on the ship and tell them Mike was still alive and I was hanging on to the promises of God! I was clinging to hope. It was me and God and Mike.

Here we are at the dirt floor hospital with the nurse that only had one syringe. She kept this in her pocket unsheathed. I wondered what kind of terrible disease Mike could get from this poor hygiene—then thought of the phlebotomist who rode off on her bicycle with the blood samples in the basket on the front of her bicycle. I began praying for Mike not to contract some horrible disease from all this poor hygiene, assuming he lived.

The interpreter explained that the doctor thinks Mike had or is going to have a heart attack. They want to move him to the hospital in Cancun, 45 minutes away. An ambulance was not required but recommended. *How much for ambulance ride?* $800. *Oh my!*

If you have ever cruised, you know that on the ship, you use a sea pass card tied to your credit card. That is because there is no cash allowed to be used on board. You have cash for when in port, but typically you do not need much. Because of that, we did not keep much cash at all. As we were leaving the ship, our new son-in-law, Rory Siren, shoved $200 in my hand and said you may need this. So this was the only cash we had. The hospital in Playa del Carmen was on the daily cash program; however, they accepted our credit card as daily payment. Now we should have had travel insurance. We purchased it for every trip we had taken to that point, and we have done so every time since. But this time, the purchase slipped through the cracks because of the intensity of so many moving parts of a destination wedding. So, that meant they collected their daily rate of $2,500 each day. They also collected for the blood draw each time. This was

$40, which Dr. Love ended up paying because the bike rider phlebotomist wanted cash. The hospital put the rest on our credit card. $800 was being requested for the ambulance. That would be cash only, which I did not have. So, I asked what is my other option: he said a taxi. How much? $45 American; sold! Call a taxi.

While we were waiting for the taxi to arrive, Mike wanted a shower, and I went to town to see about getting something to eat which was a big mistake! I could not pull off finding something that seemed suitable to me and make the money thing work. I had only American dollars, and they wanted pesos. Soon I was surrounded by a group of young men who seemed very interested in my cash. That got me scurrying back to my safety oasis in the hospital. When I returned, there was quite the chaos. While Mike was taking a shower, he had pulled the IV from his arm. Blood began to squirt everywhere in the bathroom! This brought attention and more Spanish words I had never heard before. Finally, we got things settled down and were ready for the taxi ride to Cancun.

The taxi driver comes and gets his instructions in Spanish from the hospital, and his eyes get as big as saucers! He pulls away with us in the back like a bat out of you know where. We made it to Cancun in record time! We are at the hospital in Cancun that looks like a hospital back home! The next part of our journey begins in dos minutos...

Chapter 13.

The Manuscript

We got back home to Fort Wayne on a flight with all the kids that were on the cruise. I was feeling great. I had a business trip to an important meeting in Naples, Florida, the next day. In considering whether to go, my logic was, maybe God had healed me. Maybe, what the Mexican cardiologist thought had happened, was inaccurate. But either way, I seemed fine and decided to go to Naples.

Sherry and I flew to Orlando, where she stayed to visit with her sister. I drove by myself the four hours to Naples. I then spent four days in meetings, then drove back to Orlando. Then Sherry and I flew home. The next day, we went to Kendallville (about 40 minutes from our house) to meet with our attorney, Doug Atz.

We drove back to the house, and I went upstairs. Sherry was with me. Suddenly, I had pain in my chest that hurt so bad, I could not move or talk. I had no idea such pain existed. Or that you could survive for more than a few seconds with that much intense pain. I was frozen in position with my arms vertical against my chest. Sherry began to try to get me to talk, and I could not. Shortly she called 911, and the ambulance came to take me to the ER.

Approximately sixty seconds after she called, there was a knock at the door. It was an EMT who lived across the street. He had heard the call and came immediately. Coincidence? Or the mercy of God? The EMTs transported me to the nearest hospital, a block down and across the street from our house.

When they started working on me, the EMT and Sherry continued to try to get me to talk. Finally, I forced out a word that was an explosion of air and no voice. PAIN, PAIN. As I said above, I had no idea that kind of pain even existed. It went on and on and on. It never decreased, but it did get worse. I was praying, "Lord, if it is my time to go, I am ready to go, but is this pain necessary?" God spoke to me very clearly, **"If you want to share in my glory, then you must share in my suffering."**

People often ask me, "How did God speak to you?" It is hard to quantify it. When I had my NDE, which I will describe in a minute, God spoke audibly and overwhelmingly. While this speaking to me was clear, it was more like an internal voice. My reaction to that was something like, *Great! That is not what I wanted to hear.* I thought, okay, I have got another idea. How about you overwhelm me with a sense of your presence and love? Because frankly, I thought at this point in dying, I would sense you far more than I am now. God spoke very clearly to me in the same way again. **"When Jesus was on the cross, He cried out my God, my God, why have you forsaken me? If I overwhelmed you with the sense of my presence, there would be no suffering."** My reaction was, *Nooooo, I don't want to hear that.* As always, what looked a complete disaster was far from it.

Then all at once, the pain stopped. I discovered later that my heart had stopped. They had to give me the paddles three times to restart my heart. When the pain stopped, I was looking down on myself, but I was not in the ER. There was not a microsecond between life and wherever I was. As is common with people who have had near-death experiences, this seemed more real and solid than anything in normal life. It made the life on earth, by comparison, seem not substantial.

I was looking at myself kneeling at an altar. It was a wooden railing that seemed to be around 30 feet long. It went horizontal in front of me. I was in the middle, centered before a beautiful stained-glass window. As it went to my left, the railing made about a ninety-degree angle and went on toward the back of the room.

The stained-glass window was large, maybe 40 feet high and 30 feet wide. It was beautiful, and the colors were mostly red, blue, and a clear sort of color. I watched as I seemed to conclude my prayer, get up, and move to the left of the altar. There was a wall with three large windows to my left and behind where I was kneeling at the altar. They were 25 feet high and at least 10 feet wide. They did not have glass in them. The windows were open to the outside. I was looking out these windows with no fear or emotion of any kind. I do not remember any transition, but I was no longer looking at myself. It was like my soul reentered my body. I was now me, looking out those windows. I had the strong sense that I was looking out into eternity. I was not out there in eternity, but I was very close to it. It was right outside that window that had no glass in it. There was like a thin screen or veil that was like the thinnest of cloths that covered the windows. You could see through it clearly and hear everything that was going on outside.

But the screen shielded the full sensory impact of what you were looking at. Outside the window was a beautiful meadow. Framing the meadow in front of me and to the right was a forest of pleasant and inviting trees.

There were a small number of animals in the meadow, one of which was a majestic elk with a huge rack. He was standing in the middle of the meadow and seemed to be looking right at me. Behind the trees to the right, I could hear what seemed to be the ocean breaking on a beach. I was just looking. I do not remember thinking anything or feeling anything at that moment.

Suddenly, a voice spoke to me. This voice was coming from everywhere. It seemed to be coming from every molecule inside of me, in the room, and out in eternity. It was coming from everywhere. The voice spoke with absolute authority. Not with anger, but no grandma's type love in its tone. It seemed like it was asking me the most important question that had ever existed. It was like the words of a judge. I emphasize that this voice was not like the prior communications. It was more real than anyone ever speaking to me on earth. The voice said, "Are you ready for this manuscript to go the publisher?"

Suddenly, I had a lot of feelings. Sort of an "Oh my gosh" moment. I felt some fear, a small sort of panic, and I remember thinking, "Is this a trick question?" There was never a question of whether I had an option to answer. It was more than needing a breath. More than the necessity of your breath being expelled during a Heimlich maneuver.

I had to speak. I said in a somewhat fearful, somewhat anxious voice with a raised sort of anxiety. "Well, I am trusting in Jesus. I am betting everything on Him. He is my hope. So, if that is what you mean, then I am ready." That part of my answer seemed to be me. The second part of my answer, "But if you mean, have I completed everything

God created me to do, the answer is no," seemed that it was being given to me. It may have been the Holy Spirit assisting me with my answer. I cannot overstate the reality of this moment. Even many years later, it is a clearer, more solid memory than any earthly event.

Since this incident, I have heard many different pastors teach a remarkably similar lesson. It is about what we will face when we pass away. The teaching is that when we die, we will face two questions. What have you done with my son Jesus Christ? And what have you done with the time I gave you? I do not recall ever thinking about those questions in my life before that day. But since then, there has never been a day I have not thought of it. The profound depth of the question amazes me more and more as time goes on.

Once I answered the question, the voice spoke again and said, "Then live what you believe."

Instantly I was back in the ER. There did not seem to be a microsecond between the voice telling me to live what I believed and my being back in the ER—no time to contemplate what it all meant. And certainly, no further discussion.

Chapter 14.

Sherry's Take on the Days of the Manuscript

Some people say they live life in the fast lane. Mike and I did. For us, taking business trips was an opportunity to create another adventure. We would shove in visits with out-of-town family. We would sneak in a little visit to the most beautiful places in whatever part of the world we were in. It was just the norm to our way of thinking.

After we returned from the cruise and our adventure in Mexico, Mike decided he was okay to go on this business trip. That was easy for me to justify. For one reason, I was looking forward to going to Orlando. I could see my sister and brother-in-law there. That was good. I loved them both, and being back in Orlando, my hometown, was a joy.

After the trip, when we got back to Fort Wayne, our crazy schedule resumed. We went to see Mike's family attorney about the two estates he was Executor over. Then, afterwards, we went home instead of going to our office. It was not long when Mike began acting strange. He had his arms pulled up tight against his chest/abdomen area. His face was down toward his chest. His fists were tight, and he would not or could not speak.

I am trying frantically to determine what he is feeling or what is going on with him so the next move could take place. He gave no response after several times of questioning. I called 911 for an ambulance. But I could not give them the medical information they wanted because I just did not have it. Mike could not talk. It seemed like barely hanging the telephone up; our doorbell rang. It was our neighbor who was an EMT.

The EMT began to assess Mike by taking his blood pressure, pulse, oxygen levels, and other vitals. Soon, the ambulance arrived with two more EMTs who got IVs started in Mike and gave him oxygen.

They were trying to talk to Mike, talking to each other, and talking with someone at the hospital. Suddenly, the world as we had known it was all changed. Mike was transported to the nearest hospital. One that is across the street from our house. Mike went into the emergency room as a STAT, meaning he was moved up the triage to immediate care. It looked to me as though this was the heart attack. The one the ship doctor and the cardiologist from Mexico warned us about.

Mike was being worked on in an ER room. Our youngest son, Tyler, was with him in the ER room. I stood out in the lobby calling family members to notify them of the situation. I could see Tyler and Mike from where I was standing, making my cell phone calls. I could see the monitors that Mike was hooked up to. They monitored his heart, blood pressure, pulse, and oxygen levels. I saw the heart monitor flat line. I heard that horrible sounding alarm that goes off when the heart stops. I could see Tyler's face as he turned and yelled, "Come quickly, Dad died!"

As I raced down the hall toward Mike, who was getting paddled, I hear myself say with great confidence, "No, he did NOT!" As the doctors and nurses worked on Mike, I, along with Tyler and a close friend, Karen Failor, who had just arrived at the hospital, dropped to our knees. It was right in front of the ER nurse's station. We were praying. We were praying out loud. I had my eyes closed.

After a bit, I felt this hand on my right shoulder patting me and heard this voice saying, "Mrs. Nickols, he is back." This was Mike's ER doctor, who then explained that Mike had a very serious heart attack called the "widow maker." Only about 5% of the patients survive this kind of heart attack. He had, so far. This hospital did not have a cardiac cath lab, so we had to move Mike by ambulance to another hospital across town.

The doctor was not sure Mike would survive the drive or the procedure or what his life would be like if he did. All the doctors could tell me was that Mike had a bad heart attack. He would need a cardiac cath procedure so they could further assess his condition.

Mike went in the ambulance, and Tyler, Karen, and I drove to the next hospital. Once there, they got Mike immediately into the cardiac cath Lab. Mike's cardiologist put a stent in his heart. We were then sent to Cardiac Intensive Care. Mike's regular cardiologist, at this time, was the treating physician.

The next day after the heart-stopping and stent procedure, his cardiologist came to see him. He gave us this big lecture about how life was changed for us. We would have to get used to Mike being basically an invalid. Our lifestyle would require a big change. He said you need to learn to slow down—plan on getting a rocking chair to watch life from. Our days of participating in life as we have known it are over. The same feeling I had at the first hospital when informed that Mike had died came up again.

This time, I let the good doctor finish speaking. I then went to the nurse's station, where Mike's most wonderful nurse sat perched, watching over him like a hawk. This I loved. I said to her, does anyone ever "fire" their doctor? She said sure; it happens all the time. Good, I said, he is fired. We want a new doctor. This decision meant Mike started seeing the doctors that were on rotation.

There were 25 doctors in the cardiologist's practice. We could choose one from the doctors who came on rounds. I am forever grateful for the rising inside me on both occasions. I believe this was a prompting of the Holy Spirit. One reason is because Mike lived and the second one because we got a doctor who was our doctor for life!

We both think Dr. David Schleinkofer is the greatest cardiologist that ever lived! Mike was only in the Cardiac ICU for a day; they sent him to a regular room in which he rarely stayed. He felt so good. He walked around that floor faster than I did. He looked good. He seemed good. We were sent home with orders to change his diet and get regular cardiac exercise. The exercise regimen was great news for Mike as he loved exercising. The diet change was not so much fun. I was thinking that finally, this nightmare of an ordeal was behind us. Now, we can get going back to life as we knew it before. God was saying, not so fast; there is more to come.

Chapter 15.

Heart Attack Number 3

Mike

Two weeks went by, and it was a Sunday evening. I spoke on the telephone to our son, Tyler, in Sydney. Tyler had returned to school in Sydney, Australia. As I spoke to him, I started feeling the same uncomfortableness in my chest when I had the last heart attack. Then the escalating pain began ramping up. I didn't want to alarm him, so I excused myself, got off the phone, and called for Sherry.

Sherry came running, and the pain was spiking up. She called 911. The EMT that lived across the street who answered the call the last time had a wife who was also an EMT. Once again, she was at the door in less than a minute. They rushed me to the hospital across town that had a cath lab. It was late Sunday evening. At the hospital, they only had one cath lab functioning on a Sunday night.

An elderly gentleman had gone into the cath lab when we arrived. He ended up being in there for over two hours. During that time, they were giving me the highest dose of morphine and the highest dose of nitro allowed. I was semi-conscious but, would, in distress, call out, it is coming back! It is coming back! I did not have any epiphanies during this event. I remember thinking, geez, Lord, I thought we had gotten past this part! Finally, I got into the cath lab.

The next thing I remember was the cardiologist speaking to me. It seemed like I was at the bottom of a well, and he was yelling down to me. Mike, I cannot get the artery open. We are going to need to do bypass surgery, but I need your permission. I remember thinking, "exactly what choice do I have?" I said yes, and the next thing I remember was waking up in my hospital room. They had done a five-way bypass that took eight hours. Plus, three more hours of surgery to stop the bleeding. So much for that one stent.

While I was unaware of what was happening, so much had gone on in my absence. As always, being a child of God, loving Him, and desiring to be what He wants makes all things work together for good. It is a bit like the children of Israel being delivered out of slavery in Egypt. Although God had done mighty miracles and given them promises of the future, life-threatening adventures would come one after another. I just kept putting my hope in Christ.

Chapter 16.

Sherry's Take on Third Heart Attack

Two weeks later, Mike was on the phone speaking with our son, Tyler. I was asleep. Mike woke me up, saying the pain was back. I could not believe my ears. This time the uprising that came up inside me was not there. This time it felt like, oh no, not this again. I was thinking, how many times can a person go through this and still live? The words from Mike's original cardiologist were attempting to return to my mind. The words about being an invalid and watching life go by from a rocking chair.

I called 911, send the ambulance again. This time the EMT said to have him come downstairs as we had difficulty getting the stretcher down our stairs. This time the EMTs were barking at me to calm down. This time, I felt alone and hopeless. We all decided to go directly to the hospital that was further away. There was no point in going to the one across the street. His treating physician was at the one further away, and the cath lab was there. This time they wasted no time getting him there.

As I was driving alone to the hospital, I told the Lord to give me a sign of hope for Mike. I needed that because, at the moment, I was feeling pretty hopeless. The ambulance went on ahead with its lights blaring, and I got stopped at a traffic light. A car pulled up alongside me in the left-hand turn lane. I look over at the car; on the passenger window is a picture of Jesus looking right at me. I took this as the sign God sent me. It was just enough hope for the moment.

When we arrived at the ER, again, they took Mike straight back. It was a Sunday night. They explained there was only one cardiac cath lab open on Sundays and only one team. Mike was so quick in and out of the cardiac cath lab when he got his stent; I was thinking no big deal. I was wrong! This time it would be a two-hour wait!

We were in the ER with an angel of a nurse (can you tell I love and respect nurses?). She was an angel. She had complete command of the situation, which appeared to me to be completely out of control. Mike would start yelling the pain is coming back. Heather, our nurse, would come over and give him some medication. Mike would calm down for a while. The cardiologist on call was not our regular doctor. He was tall, thin, and beyond anxious. He kept calling by telephone to the cath lab, asking if we could get in there. Then he would scream, get the hell out of there; my patient is dying. He also was furious at a resident in the ER who gave Mike blood thinners upon presenting in ER. The trouble with this was that Mike was already on blood thinners and very likely could be facing a surgery. I could hear him ream the young ER doctor over that. I thought our cardiologist was going to have a heart attack.

Meanwhile, Heather, the angel nurse, was calm, smiling, and told me I had the most important job in the room. I was to keep Mike talking and awake. She said you keep talking to him and do not leave his side. As I said, this scene went on for two hours. I seriously thought there was no more any of us in that room could take when we got word the cath lab was clear. This time Mike was in the cath lab longer than the last. The cardiologist came out to tell us Mike needed bypass surgery right then. He said they had already called for a thoracic surgeon. As soon as he arrived, they would begin what would be a very long surgery.

It was a rainy and cold winter night in February. As I look up to see the surgeon come in the doorway, my heart leapt with joy. I knew this surgeon very well. When I worked for the HMO Insurance Company, this surgeon was among our most respected and skilled surgeons. I knew his work. He was the best in our area. He had a remarkable reputation. God was so good.

This time, we had almost all the adult children there while Mike was in surgery. Although it was around 4:00 a.m., there was no way for me to sleep. I wanted to pray Mike through this surgery. I settled down in a seat in the lobby with my Bible open to Psalm 91. This is the Psalm about being in the shelter of God. I really needed God to shelter me, and Mike now. Mike's brother and sisters had been there but had left for a while. The kids had all fallen asleep. They were in various chairs scattered throughout the waiting room.

I was almost numb as the day's events had taken an emotional toll on me. I look up from my Bible reading, and here comes what looks like a doctor in scrubs walking toward me. I remember thinking, do not come over here and tell me Mike died.

As he came closer, I recognized him. He was an anesthesiologist. His children attended the same Christian high school our sons had attended. He came over and said, "I wanted to come out here to tell you something. I heard the call come out that an anesthesiologist was needed. It was for emergency surgery on a Michael Nickols. So, I volunteered to come."

He added, "I began praying the minute the call went out, and I will be with him, praying constantly during the surgery." This comforted me more than words can say. God was being so good to us. I felt very much covered by His wings, as it says in Psalm 91.

After about a half hour, a nurse comes out with a bag in her hand. She said she wanted me to have Mike's wedding ring. She placed the bag in my hand. As she was leaving, she said all is well with Mike. She, too, would be covering him in prayer. The long vigil began. After eight hours, they sent word that Mike was out of surgery. The doctor said it was 5-way bypass. He said his heart is damaged because of three heart attacks. But we must wait for about three months to see the extent of that damage. Then while Mike was in the recovery room, the surgeon had to take him three more times into surgery to stop the bleeding. He was alive. It was going to be a long recovery. That was all the surgeon could tell me.

Chapter 17.

After Bypass - Mike

I now had tubes going everywhere, and several machines hooked up to me. There was constant beeping and endless poking. I was as weak as a kitten and gray as ash. Someone had to help me with all the activities of daily living. The hospital stay was 21 days. Sherry had worship music playing 24/7 in the room. She would not let anyone be negative, fearful, or sad in the room.

One day, Frank, the man who had led me to the Lord, came to see me. Sherry greeted him in the hall and told him, "Mike does not look good, but you need to be incredibly positive in his presence."

Frank said, "He could handle it, no problem." He walked in the room, took one look at me, burst into tears, and ran out into the hall.

I looked and felt very bad. In fact, it was questionable if I would recover. And if I did, what would that look like? After 20 days in the hospital, they said I could go for a walk outside of the restricted area of my room and the area right by the nursing station, an extremely limited area. I was so glad to get the chance to expand my territory. I talked Sherry into us going to the cafeteria. By the time we got there, I wanted to call an ambulance to take me back! I remember a few moments of a few days, but Sherry's recollection is crystal clear.

Chapter 18.

After Bypass - Sherry

Hospitals are great when you need them, but they are no place to be for rest. Hospitals are noisy, busy, and there is never enough nursing staff. Things are going on all the time, especially on the cardiac care floor.

As it turned out, the very day Mike had his bypass surgery, someone else we knew had a heart attack. He was the father of our sons' friend from their Christian school when they were in high school. He had had a heart attack the same day Mike had the second one. On the day Mike had his third attack, their dad had his second.

He was working late at night alone. He had a heart attack with no one to help him, and he died. This made me more determined than ever not to leave Mike's side. It also caused me to put some strict guidelines over his care. We were not going to tell this news to Mike at this time. I kept a close watch on his heart.

When Mike finally opened his eyes, his first words were, "What is the plan?" I said the plan is for you to get well. I never left Mike for the next 21 days except for one night. Mike's doctor said if I did not go home and sleep in my own bed, he would admit me to the hospital in another room away from Mike. I must have looked like a patient to him. Mike's older sister, Pam, was a trooper; she stayed with us almost every day and night. Our kids were great; every one of them was putting in their all to help.

During these days, our oldest daughter seemed especially attentive. Her commitment was strong to be a help but also in learning. She later became a RN saying she felt called to the profession because of Mike's hospitalization. At that time, we only had two grandchildren, Anna Rose and Micah Nickols.

Anna Rose was about two years old at the time of Mike's surgery. We were very close to her, and her to us. She really wanted to see her Papa. I was genuinely concerned because of her young age and how Mike looked with all the tubes and machines; he just did not look himself. But her mom and dad said no, she can see him. So, we all tried to prepare her for a vastly different-looking Papa than the one she had seen just a couple of days ago.

She walked right in that hospital room straight to Papa's bedside. She put her little 2-year-old toddler hand on top of his chest with tubes and monitors everywhere. She then boldly declared, "Because Jesus lives in your heart, He will heal your heart."

More hope, God was sending through the best hope army He had. I kept a very tight structure on Mike's recovery. When they first brought Mike back to his room from recovery, they said he should get up and walk in a couple days. They were hoping to send him home in about 5 to 7 days. I was thinking, no way! If you take one look at this man, he looks dead. He was gray, weak, and barely conscious. They gave him some pain medicine with codeine in it. It was no time until we discovered he was allergic to that. He began to hallucinate and get combative. Thankfully, being used to being with patients in the hospital, I thought it was his medication, but was sure glad to get confirmation that was exactly what was causing the odd symptoms. They took him off that, and all he could have was regular strength Tylenol.

Mike had an incision in his chest that was downright scary. It probably was made worse because of having to go back in his chest three times to stop the bleeding. He also had about 3 inches long incisions down his leg from his groin to his ankles. This is where they took the veins for the bypass. He had lost his entire body weight of blood and had to receive many transfusions. (I actually thought this might be an answered prayer, too, from the time he was in the Mexican hospital with the community syringe being used).

Every day, those wounds needed wound care. The nurses were teaching me how to do it. It made me feel sick. We had to keep compression tights on his leg where they took the veins. Pulling those things over those wounds was about all I could take. I bathed him, fed him, got him up to go to the bathroom. I later learned that they had forgotten a few things when they gave us the discharge timeframe. They had not considered his three heart attacks and total blood replacement.

Nonetheless, Mike was not progressing the way they hoped he would. Throughout the night, he would open his eyes wide and gasp for air every 10 minutes. All day and all night every day, for now, the third day of his recovery, this took place. I was going on virtually no sleep for several days, just cat naps. Mike was about the same, awake every 10 minutes.

The next morning on rounds, we got a different cardiologist. That is what happens when you are an inpatient. You would see all the doctors in the practice. This doctor mentioned Mike's gasping episodes as normal and would pass. I said, "No, it is not normal. If you give me 30 seconds of your undivided attention, I will act out what he does." He did give me those few seconds, and I acted out what Mike was doing.

Immediately, he said he knew exactly what it is. He said the treatment to correct it is very risky as it can cause sudden blood pressure loss, and we may lose him. At this point, letting him continue to drown from cardiac failure was not really an option, so we agreed to go for the treatment.

Here I was again, needing a strong dose of hope from the Lord. About that time, a nurse who we had not yet met walked in. She was upbeat, fresh, seemed confident but not arrogant at all. She had a wonderful relational personality.

As she was preparing the treatment which they would deliver by IV, she was talking away. I asked her about the treatment if she had done this before. She was like, yes, ma'am. She told us this was going to go fine. She said I am a Christian and never do anything, but most especially this, without giving this over to God. She was right. The treatment went great, and it worked! Mike was finally able to get some rest. He had been drowning. His chest was filling up with fluid, and his heart could not pump it out, so Mike was drowning in fluid. Thank God for the doctor He sent on rounds. And the nurse who was scheduled that day. God is faithful.

Mike did not go home in a week. This was a tough slog pushing through this recovery. About the end of the second week, Mike began to get ornery. I took this as a good sign. Still, no one was allowed in the room with any strife, negativity, or looks that would tell Mike he looked like death. I had Darlene Zschech worship music playing 24/7. The nurses were great, just not enough of them. We had lots of visitors. Many people from all over the world prayed. Our kids were amazing. They were so supportive of both of us.

Our youngest daughter, Melissa, was pregnant with her first child as all this was happening. She was not feeling great herself, but she was a servant, nonetheless. She really could have used her mom during this pregnancy, but much of the time, she was toughing it out on her own.

One day while visiting Mike, she had to be rushed to the ER. Our daughters went the extra mile to do anything and everything that needed to be done. We owned our own business. Our oldest daughter worked there at the time, and she had the brunt of business decisions fall on her. She never missed a beat. All our kids pitched in with all they had to give. It was a scary day after 21 days when they said we were going home. I was thankful to have the backup and all the monitors at the hospital. It brought me comfort. By this time, Mike was getting very restless to get moving again. He never complained. He had to be in tremendous pain, but never a word about the pain. He was determined to get well, and so was I.

I truly felt the prayers and God's grace taking us through this.

Chapter 19.

Post Bypass - Mike

The first thing I remember after getting out of the hospital was a week later, going to the rehab. Back when they implanted the stent, I was on the bikes, other equipment and doing all the exercises right out of the gate. Now the best I could do was to take one small step on a two-step stair box and then step down. I was like a little old man. The funny thing was, though, I never felt despair or fear about the future. I knew God had spared me for a mission that He had planned from the earth's foundation. He has a mission like that for you as well.

From the foundation of the world, God has wanted every person to come to Him. He desires to restore all that the world, the flesh, and the devil have stolen from you. God's ways often do not line up with our ways. I would not have imagined having a third heart attack, especially after hearing God's message to me on the other side. So being almost dead again and a long road to recovery was confusing, to say the least. Yet, I always had an extraordinarily strong hope and assurance that I would recover and be about the business of the Kingdom of God.

I pushed hard every day to do more than they said I could or should do. I was driven to get back to full steam. And I did. Sherry was like an angel from heaven. I should have died at least three times. But her constant care and commitment to getting me well saw me through. I have never experienced such love expressed in self-sacrifice.

It took me a few months to sort of recover. I remember the first time I went back to church; I was so gray, I scared almost everyone who saw me. I was thinking, "what is wrong with you people" I was so happy to be there. When I had the second heart attack, and the pain was so great, I told God I was ready to go but asked if the pain was necessary. His answer was basically yes, it is.

As I shared above, I clearly heard Him say, *if you want to share in my glory, you must share in my suffering.* My reaction was no; I didn't want to hear that. I had another idea. I told him, "How about overwhelming with your presence? I was expecting you to feel much closer at this time." God clearly said to me, "When Jesus was on the cross, He called out my God, my God, why have you forsaken me?" I remember not wanting to hear that right before my heart stopped, and I was on the other side.

This part of the journey was necessary as well. So, it is with you. God will use every bit of your pain to grow your intimacy with Him, even if it is self-inflicted. And to prepare you to fulfill the destiny He created you for. Despite being weak and gray in color, our life began to explode in growth. The doors of ministry began to swing wide open for us.

Chapter 20.

Post Heart Attack - Sherry

Mike's recovery after the second heart attack was not even a recovery. He felt better than he had before! The recovery after this third heart attack would be long and difficult. We went to cardiac rehab three to five days a week. Our big argument was whether he was going to drive or not. He was not supposed to drive for six weeks. Well, that did not happen. He started driving almost immediately.

My focus was completely on his recovery. Our health insurance business was taking a hit. We had about 17 employees at the time. Our daughter, Aimee, was making the business's day-to-day decisions and helping with our house and Mike's recovery. Our daughter, Melissa, was working there also. Melissa was pregnant with her first child. She was having to make a myriad of adjustments. She was in her first year of marriage, pregnant, working and helping me with Mike. This was difficult as I was not there for her as much as I would have liked for all the changes she was going through.

These days held many challenges of all types. Because we were gone from our business, some employees became discouraged. One by one, resignations began coming in. In their defense, it did look like Mike was a long shot for a recovery. He was such a strong force in the business, it seemed unlikely anyone could fill his shoes. In the natural, all signs pointed to the fact that our lives as we had known them before would never return.

During the next three months, the only employees left were our daughters. Mike was itching to get back to work, so we returned part-time. For me, it was quite difficult to get back in the workflow. We had lost most of our staff. Our clients were quite concerned about Mike. I am sure some were sincere, but most were uncertain where it left their business if he did not make it. At the same time as his recovery, legislation on healthcare reform began picking up steam. It was a perfect storm for us in our business. Between Mike's health and healthcare reform legislation, our business deteriorated. We would survive both. God made a way.

One day at lunch, our oldest daughter said she wanted to talk to us about something. She said that she felt called to be a nurse while Mike was in the hospital. She wanted to go back to college and get her nursing degree. She wanted to move back home while she went to school. This meant she would leave the business on a full-time basis. She was still single at this time. We are always elated when our kids' answer God's call. It was comforting having her at home. While we started out with a full house, it had thinned out by this time.

Mike's birthday is May 19th. This birthday was one for the books for sure! On May 18th, our daughter Melissa and her husband Rory had their first child, a daughter, Gabrielle Elaine. It was quite the celebration! Another grandchild, and this one has my middle name (and her mom's), Gabrielle Elaine, and Mike made it to his birthday!

As Mike improved, I spent more time with our daughter Melissa and our new granddaughter Gabby. Aimee got into nursing school. Matt was growing his family and business. Craig, Cory, and Tyler were away from home attending college. Life had changed, but we were returning to the pace of it again.

I so wanted Mike to be well, and he was getting better daily. We had three grandchildren, and being Grandma was the best gig ever! We were working in the business again five days a week. It was not long that it was breakneck speed again!

We were attending church at a local church, Calvary Temple. The new pastor and his wife were a refreshing lift for that church. They asked us to open a coffee house in the church. We knew little to nothing about coffee houses. Mike, ever the adventurer, saw this as an avenue to bring the Hillsong-type worship into the church in Fort Wayne, which he felt called to do. So, we spent time and money building the coffee house into the centerpiece of the church.

For anyone that knows Mike, if he is anything, he is passionate. As I write this, the memories of this moment in time are not as vivid as the others. We had so many irons in the fire, so to speak, life was a blur for me.

Chapter 21.

Ministry After My Near-Death Experience

As Sherry mentioned, Pastor Bill Campbell and his then-wife Sherri asked us to start a coffee shop at the church. This was when most people were afraid to talk to me. I looked so close to death.

When we got the coffee shop going, it seated over 50 people. It had a decked-out kitchen. We had the fancy Italian expresso machines and nice display cases. Our shop served all kinds of specialty drinks as well as regular coffee. We had tons of rolls, donuts, muffins, and other things. But the most important thing was we had an exceptionally large screen TV right in the middle of the counter. You could view it from every spot in the cafe.

Every second we were open, we played Hillsong Worship on that TV. Mostly it was worship recorded at Hillsong conferences live from Sydney, Australia. At the conference, there would be over 30,000 people in the super dome from all over the world worshiping God. These images caught people's attention as this was not common in most churches in America.

People in the coffee house would stand mesmerized in front of the video on that large screen TV. Hardly anyone had ever seen worship like that. Our church was around 1,500 people. We were determined to expose everyone to the kind of worship I knew God had called me to back in 1983. The coffee shop thrived, as did the hunger for worship that grew out of our place of fellowship.

Soon, Sherry and I took over the usher's ministry at the church as laypeople. Then they added in greeters. Then first-time visitors, then prayer team. It just continued until we had 11 ministries and 150 people under the umbrella, which we called Day Maker Ministry.

God was using us like we had always wanted Him to. Physically, I was getting stronger but still in the process of recovery. The church hired a new worship leader and his wife, Benny, and Kelli Ferguson, who both had a heart for worship like Sherry and I did.

For three years, we served together, changing the culture of the church. Tyler, our youngest son, was in Australia going to Hillsong College. One day while he was in class, Brian Houston, the founder and Senior Pastor of Hillsong church and ministries, asked the class a question. "How many in here are from England, how many from California, how many Sweden?" Tyler called out, "How about Fort Wayne, Indiana?"

It was a big laugh at that moment because no one knew of Fort Wayne. But after class, Brian Houston, who at that time was the Senior Pastor at Hillsong, approached Tyler and said, "The Hillsong team is going to be in America in the summer. We need another place to minister between Detroit and Chicago? Are you near either of those cities?" Tyler told him we were. Brian told him to call Mark Zschech, Darlene Zschech's husband (at that time, the head of all worship at Hillsong worldwide), and talk to him about the Hillsong Worship team coming to Fort Wayne. Tyler was very reluctant to call, but I kept after him.

When he finally did call and later meet with Mark, Mark was very non-committal and said don't call me; I'll call you. So, after a few weeks of no response, I wrote Mark Zschech a letter. He wrote back to me and said he would like to get together when I was in Australia.

Sherry and I started planning our first trip to Australia that day. We had won a trip to Hawaii before my heart attacks, and the trip was scheduled at the time when I was so weak, we could not go. The company we were going with, World Insurance, gave me $5,000 for a trip of our choosing because I could not go on the trip at the time the insurance company had it planned. That paid all most all our trip to Australia. We did meet up with Mark and Darlene Zschech.

While it took a few months, Mark and Darlene worked with us to schedule the Hillsong Worship team to come to Calvary Temple, the church we attended at that time. It was an electric moment, but the required preparation was unbelievable.

Five of our kids participated like it was a full-time job. Tyler could not be a part of it because while the Hillsong Worship team was doing worship events around America, he attended Hillsong Leadership College in Australia.

Benny and Kelli totally gave themselves to preparing for the worship event. We had scores of people working on it for weeks. We had no broadcast equipment or expertise at our church. This was significant because we wanted to project the worship on the screens. We also wanted to have an overflow room. Benny found a way. We set up an overflow room for 1,500 where they could hear and see the service live. We wired it and set up the cameras and the movie-sized screen. We wanted the intelligent lighting (moving headlights) that illuminates concerts, but we did not have them set up for our services.

God provided. There were about 40 people on the Hillsong team that came from Australia. They all had to be fed and housed. Our daughter Aimee made that all happen. Later, Darlene Zschech said their team had received the best hospitality of any city in America in Fort Wayne, IN!

All the marketing had to be done, and we were not very experienced at it. Kelli worked magic with that. We needed a trained choir and several musicians ready to go for prime time. Benny again pulled it off. We managed a crowd of 5,000 lined up wanting on 2,000 seats. Our son Matt led that team with humor and innovation. And the list goes on. The Calvary Temple sanctuary seated 2,000. But we crammed 2,700 in the building where we hosted the event and had 1,800 in the overflow that seated 1,500, and we turned away around 1,000 people. I do not know if it changed the city, but it certainly changed many of us.

Another amazing story of God's guidance and protection from those days. We went on a Royal Caribbean Cruise with most of our family and several friends. At that time, Bill Campbell, the Senior Pastor at Calvary Temple, his wife Sherri, Associate Pastor Mark and Renita Ellington, and the worship pastors Benny and Kelli Ferguson.

As usual for us, this trip was full of adventure! There was a special highlight that truly bonded us together for the ministry that was ahead. One port of call was Barbados. We think Barbados is truly one of the most beautiful places on earth! Crane Beach in Barbados is considered one of the five most beautiful beaches in the world. It has the bluest water and the softest brilliant white sand with a magnificent cliff as a backdrop where the waves crash against it. It is just a breathtaking view!

In trying to show everyone the most we could have Barbados in just one day, we saved the best for last, Crane Beach. We arrived later than we had hoped, around 2 pm. We had lunch reservations at the restaurant, which took an hour. So, we did not get to the beach until 3:00. We were supposed to be back on the ship at 5:30. It would set sail at 6 pm sharp with or without us. It takes 45 minutes to get from Crane Beach to the cruise port. That means the very latest you could leave and make it was 4:45. I planned to get on the road by 4.

Crane is a bewitching place. No one wanted to leave except Sherry and I, who knew the potential danger. We finally started back at 4:30. Still enough time if there are no delays. We had rented and were driving five jeeps in a caravan. Soon we were in a traffic jam. After 20 minutes of hardly moving at all, prayer became, for all of us, intense! We crept along and crept along. 5:30 came and went. 5:45 came and went.

At 5:55, we could see the ship but were still a few blocks away. There is an inlet from the sea that was in front of us. The ship was beyond it to the left. There was a bridge on the street we were on. It was closed due to construction. There were no bridges to the left. There was just water like a canal that went straight to the sea about five blocks down. I needed to turn right and go a block to the next bridge, but in a panic, I turned left. I was followed by four other jeeps with a bunch of panicked people in them.

As soon as I turned, I realized my mistake. So, I turned left again at the first street. It wound around and dead-ended. There was a canal on the left that went into the inlet. Four jeeps behind me. At the dead end, I tried to shift into reverse, but the transmission froze. I said out loud, that's it; we're stuck with 20 people in Barbados. In my frustration, I was unaware of my surroundings. In front of me was a guy standing in the road by his car. He asked me if I would like to use his cell phone. I said, "Who am I going to call?"

He said, "How about the ship?"

I said, "There is no way to call the ship. If there is even a phone number, how would you get it?"

Out of nowhere, a man in a small fishing boat in the canal says loudly to us. "I can get the captain on the cruise ship on my ship-to-shore radio."

I said sarcastically, "You can get the Captain of the Serenade of the Seas on that radio?"

He said, "Yes, I can."

"Well then," I said, "call him up!"

"What do you want me to say?"

"Ask the Captain if he will hold the ship. Tell him we are coming!"

The fisherman in the small boat did it; he got the Captain of the Serenade of the Seas on his radio! The captain asked how many of us there were. We said 20. The Captain on the Serenade of the Seas said he would wait 10 minutes for all of us to get on board. The man with the cell phone spoke up, saying he would take those of us in my jeep that was no longer drivable to the pier.

We, in his car, led the way for the others. We had to leave our broken-down jeep at the canal with the fisherman who called the ship for us. We all piled in the man with the cell phone's small car and took off toward the ship. Our son Matt was in the fifth jeep and was around the bend, so he could not see what was happening. He had no idea what had happened when suddenly, here we came roaring past in a new vehicle with some strange man driving. He yelled, "What is going on?" I waved and said just follow us.

The man's cell phone came in handy. We called the jeep rental company. They said they would get the broken-down jeep. The rental car company also said to leave the other four cars at the pier. They would pick them up later. We got to the pier and ran to the ship. The captain blew the horn at our arrival, and scores of people at the rail applauded and cheered.

Sherry and I have been back to Barbados at least five times. We always go to the site where this happened. Never once has there been a boat. Never once has there been a car. Never has there been even one person in that area. God miraculously made a way where there was no way. On this trip, there is no way to express the faithfulness God had displayed to us in things both large and small. He wants to do that for you. He has promised to do it for everyone who loves Him and desires to fulfill the purposes God created you for.

The cruise ship returned to San Juan two days after the Barbados adventure. Our cell phones started working again as we were in the United States. As soon as our cell phones came on, Bill Campbell, the Senior Pastor, got a call from home. It was not good news for our church.

Each year at Easter, Calvary Temple had a big Easter production called the Life-Giver. It was previously known as The Living Cross. This had been continuously performed at Calvary Temple for 25 years. There were 15 performances each year and an attendance of over 30,000.

While we were gone, several lead vocalists, actors, and actresses had quit. Contracts for equipment and marketing had fallen through, and those in charge at home wanted to cancel the event. There was a total of 23 people with us on the cruise. Twenty of them had survived the almost-miss-the-ship-in-Barbados episode! Three of our total travelers came back to the ship earlier in Barbados and missed all the fun.

Upon hearing this news about the Life-Giver, everyone felt bad for what was happening to the Easter production at our church. Not everyone attended Calvary Temple, but all of them wanted to have a meeting to see what could be done to save the Easter production. We had a meeting to discuss it. Not one of us had ever been involved with the Easter production before. However, the friendships and bonding God had put together made us all want to be a part of the solution.

In that meeting, we all committed to do all we could as individuals and as a group to make it work. When we got home, we all served together like war buddies. It was one of the best runs ever for the Life-Giver. It was such fun and a lot of super hard work with practices and shows.

My sister, Pam, and her husband, Dennis, were with us on the cruise and committed to be part of the Life-Giver production. They lived an hour and a half away from church. They drove it several times each week for two months for practices, then the 15 performances. My brother-in-law, Dennis Pratt, was selected to play the part of Satan in the production. He was the best Satan Calvary Temple had ever had! Some of us on that fateful cruise played disciples, angels, prop people, and singers. Our Granddaughter, Anna, played the part of the dead girl Jesus brought back to life.

It was just a wonderful time for the Life-Giver and for our family and friends. God used the Barbados event to build the Life-Giver team's commitment and bonding. He used what looked like an absolute disaster in Barbados to make lifelong ministry partners and friends. This began doing life with people who hungered and thirsted after God. We certainly did not accomplish this. God did it in a way no one would have dreamed He would. He is doing that for you as we speak. Put your trust in Him. Seek Him with all your heart. Do life with those that love Him. This is where the gold of life is found. It is the pearl of great prize. It is what your soul longs for. Cast yourself completely on Him no matter what your life looks like. He will turn it into something amazing.

Chapter 22.

Envision

We first had the revelation that God wanted us to bring the Hillsong-style worship to our area when we returned to Calvary Temple and Bill Campbell came to be the Senior Pastor. He came from First Assembly of God in Fort Myers, Florida.

After Bill had settled in, Sherry and I went to talk to him about our vision to bring Hillsong-style worship to Fort Wayne. He was 100% for it, and we set off on a joint mission to bring it to pass.

During the next four years, a great deal was accomplished in pursuing the vision. As I described above, we brought the Hillsong Worship team from Sydney, Australia, to Calvary Temple in Fort Wayne. People were there from many churches in the area. This began the worship revival in Fort Wayne and the surrounding communities.

We continued to model worship at church, and people began entering God's presence in a new and powerful way. Our church, Calvary Temple, began to grow. Later, Bill Campbell, the Senior Pastor of the then Calvary Temple, began to realize that God had given him callings and responsibilities beyond the vision Sherry and I had presented to him. Those additional responsibilities and callings sometimes conflicted or competed with what we were so passionate about bringing to pass.

Sherry and I and our family wanted to be fully focused to bring the original vision we had of Hillsong-type worship and ministry to our area. This caused some bumpy days for all of us. Over time, we were sent out from Calvary Temple to plant a church that would continue our calling to be all about bringing the Hillsong-type worship vision to Ft. Wayne. This also allowed Calvary Temple and Bill Campbell to freely pursue God's callings for them. The times and seasons are in God's Hands; they are not forever on this earth. But while we are in them, we must do our best to be and do what God has for that time.

Our family began a new church called Envision Life Center. I was officially ordained to the ministry as the Senior Pastor. Sherry and I pastored Envision for ten years, from 2005 to 2014. All that time, we stuck to the goal of bringing Hillsong-style worship and ministry to the Fort Wayne area.

In pursuit of that, we did many citywide worship events. We would have 20 churches or more doing a three-hour set together of Hillsong-style worship. We hired great sound and lighting companies and did it like we had observed in Australia. Usually, we would have 1,300 people or more worshiping like they never had before. We did monthly worship nights at the local university, Indiana Purdue Fort Wayne. It brought all the student ministries together for worship one night a month. There were many other events we did all over the area. The result was that people experienced God's presence instead of just going through the motions.

We were not the only ones who ushered in the renewal of worship in our area, but we made a significant contribution. We continued to be fed by our continual trips to Australia. Sherry and I went five times, and four of those times, we went to Hillsong conferences.

For so many years, in trying to answer the call of God, we had tried everything to keep the family in authentic corporate worship. We wanted to do life with people who truly hungered and thirsted after God. But for so many years, it had been exceedingly difficult. It seemed like a desert in most important areas of life. After my near-death experience, the desert bloomed. We were around so many people who hungered and thirsted after God. Our worship experience took us and so many others into the presence of God multiple times each week. In the early years of Envision, all six of our kids had roles they played. And every one of them made significant contributions to Envision and, more importantly, to the Kingdom of God. Over time, marriage, kids, and business necessities took them all in different directions. They each left in their own time spread over the later five years.

Chapter 23.

Heart Failure - Mike

About eight years after my near-death experience, I began to have trouble breathing. At first, they thought it was asthma, but it continued to worsen and would not respond to treatment.

One night, my breathing got so bad, Sherry took me to the ER. There they said I should be dead but was somehow alive. God preserves us for our destiny when we belong to Him.

After a couple of days in the hospital, it was determined that the pumping capacity of my heart had dropped dramatically. This was due to the damage from my heart attacks eight years before. My ejection fraction had dropped to 22. A normal person's ejection fraction is 60-70. That means with each pump of the heart, 60-70% of the blood is pumped out of the heart. After my three heart attacks, my ejection fraction had been in the mid-40s for eight years. Anything below 35 makes you vulnerable to your heart suddenly stopping. So, with my ejection fraction at 22, they inserted an implantable defibrillator and a pacemaker. That, combined with changes in medicine, allowed me to regain more strength and endurance than I had had since the heart attacks.

From what should have been a rocking chair level of disability, I was miraculously restored to vigor. Some people at Envision wanted to do a softball team, and I ended up coaching and pitching. At Envision, that went on for three years.

Chapter 24.

The End of Envison

We came to the 10th anniversary of Envision Church. We had seen hundreds of people become Christians. We had baptized hundreds. We did scores of weddings, funerals, and child dedications. We had taken five short-term mission trips to Haiti and had raised over $100,000 for work in that country. We had sent out four full-time missionaries to Thailand with Destiny Rescue. Saving children and women from sexual slavery. We poured thousands of dollars into the poor amongst us. We did marriage counseling, helped several people in prison get reestablished in the community. However, the main mission that we focused on for ten years of bringing the revived worship experience to Fort Wayne was completed.

Fort Wayne was full of the worship and fellowship we believed God had asked us to bring to our community. That had been what gave us passion. It was what grew the church. Through many circumstances, we began to seek God about the way forward. We asked for guidance, and guide us He did.

The changes in the healthcare industry brought about by the Obama Administration undermined our business. Our income began to fall precipitously. Our business's ability to pay the rent and utilities for the church evaporated. Then several key leaders felt it was time to move on to other pastures. We had always encouraged people to follow God and the destiny He gave them, but at this time, it was a significant event in our ability to continue.

As I have mentioned earlier, over 90% of our church people were under 30, many under 20. As time passed, they married, had kids, and took different jobs. Once the purpose of our existence was fulfilled, the drawing power to young people faded. Someone once asked a character in a book, "How did you go bankrupt?" The answer was "slowly at first and then all at once." This describes the end of Envision.

So, the formal Envision Church ministry came to an end. In many ways, however, it lived on. It reminded us of the scripture in John 12:24. *I tell you the truth unless a kernel of wheat is planted in the soil and dies, it remains alone. But its death will produce many new kernels-a plentiful harvest of new lives.*

Thirty people that had been at Envision are leading worship today. This is happening in different ministries all around the world. Also, we have several from Envision that are pastoring. So, the seed went into the ground, and much fruit is still being produced. It is a total God thing.

At that time, it did not seem like a good thing. Sherry and I had invested all our retirement savings to make Envision work for ten years. It seemed like a colossal failure on a lot of levels. There was pain as the reality dawned on us. And even greater pain in the execution of shutting down. Like the other setbacks and seeming tragedies, when we run to Christ when we trust Him in the dark, He makes all things work together for good.

Near the end of Envision, we were still trying to understand where God was taking us. The building we were leasing had a big change in plans, and we could no longer have the space. So, if we were to continue, we would have to move. We were looking around for a place to meet, and I ran into a guy I had known for a long time who owned many properties. He said he owned a church building that was rented to a church that was moving out. They had outgrown his facility. He told us to look and see if it would work for us.

We went to look at the church, and while there, we met the Senior Pastor, Kyle Mills, and the church administrator Nicole Walker from the church that was moving out, Elevate City Church. We spent a couple of hours together, and we had great fellowship. This meeting opened the door for our next ministry season at Elevate City Church.

Chapter 25.

Ministry Post Being on the Other Side - Sherry

As Mike mentioned above, transition was on the move within us. Mike felt called to bring the Hillsong-style worship to our city. Everyone who knew us knew that about us. We knew we had to complete the assignment God had given us. Because of the sense that our mission was no longer the same mission as Calvary Temple and Pastor Bill Campbell, they sent us out with their blessing to plant our own church. This began Envision Church.

We ministered at Envision for ten years. Again, thank God for our children, all six of them, and their families. They were tremendous.

Aimee and Brad raised their kids at church. I often would walk in during worship practice to see their precious girls, Olivia or Avari, sound asleep on the platform as Aimee and Tyler were practicing with the worship team. Brad worked in the tech booth doing lights and sound. Melissa, who was a young mom of two children, Gabby and Luke, at that time, did anything that was needed; her husband, Rory, who is one of the best electric guitar players ever, practiced endlessly and helped Tyler with the worship team. Tyler relentlessly networked to recruit worship team members and plan for services. Matt and his second wife, Amy, were the youth leaders for a time. Craig and Cory, although away at college at this time, did what they could to help. Keep in mind that all of us were working full-time jobs to earn money.

Envision never had anyone on payroll for the ministry. We felt God wanted us to use our business to help fund the ministry. In ten years of pastoring, much water goes under the bridge. Much joy, some tears, setbacks but so much was done to build His Kingdom on earth. We accomplished what God asked us to do. After ten years, God asked us to lay it down. We did so reluctantly. Our business had provided the building and utilities for church, and our business was headed for a drastic new direction.

As for our business at that time, Obamacare became law. It dramatically changed our business model. We went from 17 employees and 2000 agents in 40 states to just Mike and me. It seemed like the business would not survive, and it did not, but we did. With God directing our steps, He led us to move our business, scaled down to Mike and me as the only employees, to our home. We completely changed the business model to retail instead of wholesale insurance sales. Once again, God made a way. His plan was far better than ours. Then He led us to a new church, Elevate City Church.

Elevate City was a healing place for us. People at Elevate City, including our very dear new friends, Ray and Robin Prior, loved us back to health. From the moment we walked into church, it seemed we were family. Mike started a church softball team. It was a huge success. It grew from one team the first year to four teams the second year. Then we started a small group, Starting Over by Andy Stanley. It was a blessing to us and those who came. We have done that Andy Stanley small group at least 20 times! We were on the prayer team. We were greeters.

For a couple of years, we pastored over 40 small groups. We visited the sick, performed funerals and weddings. That season lasted for six years. It was some of the most fulfilling ministry we ever had. God made a way where there looked like there was no way at all.

Romans 8:28 is a living Word in both of our lives. He makes ALL things work together for good to those who love Him and are called according to His purposes. God is so good to us. All six of our children love God and are serving Him. We have thirteen Grands now! Mike not only coached softball but played softball. (So much for that rocking chair idea from the former cardiologist!) I was a softball mom. I love being Grandma and Nana, so love spending time with the Grands! Anna Rose Nickols, Micah Nickols, Gabby Siren, Luke Siren, Olivia James, Avari James, Will Nickols, Xavier Nickols, Everly Nickols, Jane Nickols, Levi Nickols, Oliver Nickols, and Stella Nickols, in their birth order. God is faithful. While life can be hard, what we know is, God is good. John 10:10. *Jesus came so we can have life to the full and overflowing; so we can enjoy our lives!* The scriptures are so right that joy, peace, purpose, and meaning are found as we fight the fight with God leading the way.

Chapter 26.

Post Envision

After we closed Envision, we started attending Elevate, and they took us in like old friends. We had over 30 people that went with us from Envision to Elevate. At first, we were just enjoying the worship and great fellowship. We served in various capacities but without a huge load on us.

After six months or so, I started a church softball program. At first, we had one team. Then two, then four. I have played and coached softball all my life. And I had many church teams, including at Envision. But this was something different. There was such bonding among the guys. For some reason, it was like so many were recapturing their mojo in life.

Life and ministry often occur in the interruptions, not in the careful plans we lay out. It is in the cracks of life that so much of value happens. The softball team was going on as softball teams typically do. We had practices and games we won and lost. But we were becoming friends.

Then a couple of events happened that changed things. Two brothers on the team lost their mother unexpectedly. And then, a couple of months later, one of those two brothers got sick and passed away very unexpectedly. The whole softball team visited the hospital, went to the funerals, provided meals, and stood with the other brother and his extended family.

During the next couple of years, as a team, we stood together through many trials and became very bonded as friends. It became one of the most powerful life-changing ministries

I have ever been involved with. Sherry was the team mom. And we had large crowds from church that came to the games. This caused the fellowship to spread and deepen.

As this grew, we decided to do a small group about starting over in life. It started with the guys and their wives from the softball team. However, before long, it grew to include many others. It was amazing that pursuing one of the loves of my life, softball, would result in such powerful ministry. Small groups have become a core of our ministry and have been life-changing for many.

As time went on, we did multiple small groups. Eventually, we ran the small group ministry with 42 groups at Elevate City Church. Our relationships allowed us to populate the small group leaders team. We also became the family pastors and, as was our style became involved in many areas of church life. During this season, we did weddings, funerals, and more hospital visits than you can count. All rose from the seed of softball and small groups that grew out of it.

During this time, business transition was ongoing, and it wasn't easy. Going from 17 employees and a 12,000-square-foot facility to Sherry and I working out of our home alone did not seem like the blessing of God in the natural. Most of our peers in the insurance business folded. Those businesses were all over the country and had many insurance agents.

Sherry and I felt God was telling us to start selling health insurance again instead of recruiting and training agents. We obeyed God, and He restored our finances. We have regained our ability to fund many things in the Kingdom of God. God, as always, making it possible to continuing fulfilling our callings.

Chapter 27.

My Beating Heart - Mike

I once heard an airline pilot describe his job as many hours of boredom interspaced with moments of terror. Our life, and the lives of people full-on after God, work similarly. The Christian life is supposed to be filled with a deepening relationship with God. That involves deepening trust. Trust in the dark. Trust when it looks like disaster. Trust when it sees we have lost or are crushed beyond repair. When all we can say is, I do not understand. It seems wrong. But because I have walked with God and seen His faithfulness, I know I can truly trust Him in what I am going through today. God always turns it around. All my life, God has been faithful. And I believe He will continue to be faithful.

It was May 23rd, 2018, 6 years after the defibrillator was implanted. Up until now, it had never gone off and shocked me. I was pitching for our softball team. A fly ball was hit to left field. It was caught, and I turned to receive the throw back into the infield. As soon as I caught the ball, extreme dizziness struck me. I bent over and then collapsed on the ground. A few seconds later, I was shocked with 360 jolts of electricity as my implanted defibrillator went off. It hit me so hard it flipped me over on the ground. I later learned that my heart had stopped from a fatal arrhythmia. The shock had restarted my heart. They called the EMS and took me to the ER. Within a few minutes, I was back to normal. The near brush with death does impact you. It makes you ask yourself a lot of questions.

Six weeks later, in the middle of the night, I got shocked again. My defib reports the results to my cardiologist right away. The next morning, they called and told me my heart had stopped again, and the defib had saved my life. Three weeks later, it happened again. And then nine weeks after that, again for the 4th time. This time at the gym. Each time, we took blood tests to try to stabilize my potassium and magnesium. They say after one or two shocks, anxiety, fear, and depression often take over. For me, I knew God was keeping me alive to fulfill the destiny He had created me for. I also knew there was purpose in the pain. That what I was going through would be of use to others if I kept my confidence in God.

My doctors were beginning to understand why it as happening, or so we thought. We added anti-arrhythmia drugs. I went 23 weeks and then shocked again. That time, I was driving into a parking lot in New Buffalo, Michigan, with some of our grandchildren in the car. I died again behind the wheel. My grandson, Micah, who was about 14 years old at the time, was in the back seat, jumped forward, and hit the brake with his hands. Sherry grabbed the steering wheel, and we stopped with no one hurt and no property damage. Once again, my defib saved my life. This added a new dimension of concern. If I was driving, others could get hurt.

After that, my doctors redoubled their efforts to stop this from happening. We added additional anti-arrhythmia drugs. After that, I went 17 months with no heart stoppage. I thought we had it licked. I had slowly gone back to driving. Sherry and I had developed a protocol where she had a cane she could use to apply the brakes, put it into neutral and pull to the side.

One night, I drove back to Fort Wayne from the Upper Peninsula of Michigan. That drive takes over 8 hours. We had been at the house less than 30 minutes. I was unloading the car from our travels. In the doorway with a suitcase in my hand, my heart stopped again. After 10 minutes, as always, I was back to normal. The closest any two shocks had ever happened was a three-week time span.

After I recovered, we felt safe to drive both of our cars to get gas in them. While I was pumping gas, my heart stopped again. Since my heart stopped twice in one day, which was unusual, we went to the ER. The cardiologist on call said he thought some of my bypasses could be clogged again. They did a cath, and one artery that had never been bypassed was clogged. This artery went straight to the area where the arrhythmias were originating. They put in a stent, and we were all extremely optimistic that now we had it solved. This happened in October. My defib device had to be replaced in December because it was time for a new battery. So, I had surgery in December to get the latest model of defibrillator/pacemaker devices implanted.

February 10th, my heart stopped again. This time while on vacation in Florida, at 4 am during my sleep. Then two days later, as we were leaving Florida to come home, it happened again. This time we were on an airplane right after take-off. Almost always, Sherry and I sit side by side on the airplane, but this time, the airline assigned us seats, one in front of the other. However, the man who sat beside me on this trip was a super great guy about my age. He turned out to be a Christian and a very mature guy. When my heart stopped, and I got shocked, he hung right in there with me, and within a couple of minutes, we just rejoined our conversation where we left off.

After this episode, it was more difficult for me to recover mentally. While we were in FL and the defibrillator went off, we went to get my blood drawn to see what my levels were. Everything was perfect. So, I knew since the tests were good this time, it meant there was pretty much nothing else that could be done, at least in my mind. But I was still alive. The fear, anxiety, and depression that comes to most people in this situation, is not from what has happened but what might happen going forward. This is so like life. So many people trade really living for fears about things that may never happen. God says 365 times in the Bible to fear not. I am going to die. My dad and mom died. Billy Graham, C.S. Lewis, and the pastor who influenced me the most died. I do four or five funerals a year. Most of them are for people younger than me. We need to be ready to go. But since we are still here, there is purpose for our lives.

Chapter 28.

Learning to Walk by Faith

I refuse to sit in a corner cowering at the thought of what might happen. I long to walk with God closer every day. Having a heart that might stop at any moment focuses the mind to pursue God's eternal plans. I love the fruit of being focused. God will reward us for billions of years for allowing Him to work through us. The sands go through the hourglass. We do not know how many grains of sand we have left. Who do we need to forgive? Who do we need to ask for forgiveness? Who can God really reach and love through me today? How can I seek Him with all my heart? Can I choose to trust Him now when I do not understand?

Based on my past experiences, my current situation, and the plans God has for me for the days I have left, what is the wise thing to do? Can I see how faithful God has been? I keep a list on my phone of God's miracles for me. Not minor stuff. Major stuff. It is over 50 items of financial miracles, healing miracles, relationship miracles. Miracles for Sherry and I and for those we love. Redemption miracles in people I was very afraid were lost forever. Miracles of provision. Sometimes, in the seven figures. Protection miracles like when we were attacked by robbers in Rome (a story for another day!) Family miracles, Church miracles, business miracles, mission miracles. Vacation miracles, friendship miracles. I must recognize how faithful He has been to me. I do not have to feign being grateful today.

Tim McGraw had a hit song with an incredibly significant line. "I hope you get the chance to live like you were dying." I get the chance to live like I am dying every day. I hope you get that chance as well. It will focus your mind on what really matters in life.

Although I walk through the valley of the shadow of death every day, God has provided for my wife and I to have an abundant life.

We did four weddings this summer. We have done three funerals this year. We travel with our kids and friends at least a couple times a year. Our son Matt provided airfare for us to go to Hawaii with 16 of our family members in April of 2021. We teach a small group every week to bring community so we all can grow as Christians. We get to do marriage counseling to help those who may be going through what we have gone through. We get to host fellowship nights and worship nights with 50 people that truly hunger and thirst after God.

God is revealing Himself in the most amazing worship events of my whole life. We get to do a food bank for the truly poor every week. We help unwed mothers who have decided to keep their babies. We believe you need to sacrifice to help the truly poor. Many of the public poor are cons. However, the widows in subsidized housing deciding between medicine and food are the really poor in America. Most people opt for an abortion because they feel they cannot take care of themselves, let alone a baby. If you are pro-life, you must intervene where you can. Do it wherever God presents opportunities for you. Loving people who can give nothing back and often disappoint us in their choices is close to real love.

The Word of God is more alive for Sherry and me in this season than ever before. My character has been strengthened, and my maturity has grown more in the last two years than in the previous twenty. It comes from focusing on knowing Him, walking with Him, and fulfilling why I am here. So, the struggles I face are a great blessing. And they are not to be compared to the amazing future on the other side God has prepared for those who love Him.

Chapter 29.

England and Alpha

In 1983, God spoke to me about the four callings on my life, as I have mentioned above. The first calling was to raise my kids to hunger and thirst after Him. To do that, I would have to do the second calling, that had two parts. First, have my kids in authentic corporate worship where they would experience God's presence. Second, have them around people who authentically walked with God so they could see what real Christianity looked like. The third calling was to use my business to build the Kingdom of God. I am well satisfied that God is fulfilling those callings. The fourth one is to treat England and Scotland like my own children. To care about their welfare and be about causing them to hunger and thirst after God.

Sherry and I have been to Scotland and England 12 times. We have tried to minister in many ways, but to be honest, it has seemed like BBs off a battleship. Very disappointing and very much unable to consider that calling realized. The last time we went to England, I went with trepidation because I was sure I would see spiritual depravity worse than before and feel so powerless to do something about it. Yet once again, our faithful God met us there.

Everywhere we went, bed & breakfasts we stayed in, the subway, tourist places, and even when we totaled our car the first day we arrived in England; everyone around us were Christian and making a real difference in their country. Near the end of our three weeks there, we were in London. We went to Hillsong London as we always had done. But we had also heard about a church called Holy Trinity Brompton. It is Anglican (Episcopalian), but we had heard it conducted church with awesome worship and an informal environment. Five thousand people were attending, and they had nine satellite locations. We decided to check it out.

The Sunday we were there was vision Sunday, and Nicky Gumbel, the Vicar (Senior Pastor), was speaking. He told about having a seminary at Holy Trinity that produced pastors and worship leaders full of life and the power of the Holy Spirit. He told about Holy Trinity's vision to take old dying congregations that the Anglican church was closing and put in Spirit-filled pastors and worship leaders from their seminary to start over in those locations.

Today, they have planted over 100 churches in the United Kingdom. I basically had nothing to do with what was happening in this revival of spiritual life in the United Kingdom. Yet, God was speaking to me loud and clear in that service. The Spirit of God was saying to me that in everything you have done to date in the Kingdom of God, it was Me doing it. You were just riding on the train. And so it is, here in the United Kingdom. It is I who does the work, people who are obedient to my calling share in the harvest and the reward of the harvest. You have kept believing in your calling. You have kept coming to Scotland and England. You have kept praying. You have kept a love for the people alive. Because of this, I am including you in the reward of this move of mine in Great Britain. Immediately, this enormous burden lifted off me. I did not know the weight of it that I had been carrying.

I had great joy and peace in the house of God that day! When Sherry and I returned home, we started financially supporting the ministry at Holy Trinity Brompton. Over time, I would get letters thanking us for the contributions. Nicky Gumbel signed them. Although I was sure they were form letters sent out to all givers, I decided to write back an email explaining how their ministry had impacted Sherry and I. Nicky wrote me back a personal email.

Shortly after this, I told him we were coming again to England for at least a month, and I wanted to spend time at Holy Trinity if that were possible. He said it was certainly possible, but he likely would not be there because he was stepping down as the Vicar after 17 years to focus full-time on The Alpha Course. I was familiar with Alpha because my sister's church had done Alpha for a few years. But I knew very little about it. When Nicky told me that, it was like a blanket of the Holy Spirit fell on me.

Nicky has been doing Alpha for over 30 years. It is being done in over 169 countries. Over 66,000 Alpha courses are going on at any given time. It is a small group where you have dinner, watch a 20-minute video of the Christian perspective on the meaning of life, and then have about 45 minutes of discussion. Millions have come to Christ through this outreach, and millions more have had their faith fortified and strengthened through this course. It is 15 sessions over 11 weeks and a weekend away and the most powerful, compelling presentation of Christianity I have ever encountered!

Sherry and I set about to learn about it and figure out how to be a part of it. Our ministry in Alpha is exploding. As we do The Alpha Course, the most common response is, my mother, sister, brother, niece, neighbor, office worker, must see this! So above what God had said were my callings; he is giving additional opportunities to be on the train He is driving! God is so good!

Chapter 30.

Lessons

Many people say in their heart; I hope that what you have been through never happens to me. That is not the life I want to live. I don't want all that trouble. No one would pick it. But what I have come to see is most people would never pick the life they are living now. The pain, the offense, the broken relationships, the experiencing the career that is not what they thought it would be. Is this all there is to life?

Surely, there is more to life than what I have experienced so far. In your life that you have now, the life you would rather not be living, lies the secret to life. Trust Jesus Christ. He has purpose in all your pain. The difference between a life that seems like hell and a life that seems like heaven is faith. Not faith in faith. Faith in the love of God for you. Faith that God sees you and clearly sees your circumstance. Faith in the wisdom of God in your situation, Faith that He truly has your best interest at heart. And finally, faith in the power of God to do what is required for you.

Recently, I was asked, how do you get that kind of relationship with God? How do you build that kind of confidence in Him? God told me in 1983 that if I wanted my kids to have a deep, authentic relationship with Him, I had to do two things. Keep them in authentic corporate worship where they would experience God's presence.

Being in God's presence in corporate worship does not just happen. Within driving distance from Fort Wayne, there are powerful worship events where thousands gather to give God glory several times a year. When I say this, I am speaking about worship events led by people with no hidden agenda, where you are worshiping God to give Him praise and be in His presence. Not to raise money or stroke the ego of someone. It takes planning and commitment to ensure you and your family are at these events. It takes sacrifice, but it is so worth it.

The second thing was to do everything I could for them to do life with people who truly hunger and thirst after God. Having a deep relationship with people will cost you something. You will offend your family and friends, and they will offend you. Forgive and keep going. Make the sacrifice to spend quality time with family, and those God is directing you to do life with. I have seen this work better than I could ever have dreamed in the life of all six of our kids. But it has also worked for Sherry and me. And it has worked for hundreds of people we have been up close and personal with in their spiritual walk. Beyond that, you must spend time regularly in God's Word. Not to be smart, educated, or to win arguments, but to have a relationship with Him and learn His heart and His ways. These things develop our relationship with God. That relationship is expressed and deepened in prayer. Not just saying prayers, not presenting our lists of "can I please have," but listening to God, praying for others, asking for eyes to see, ears to hear, and a heart like His. Be a constant forgiver. Many people are bitter and unforgiving. This will rob you of a deep relationship with God. Recognize His love and care for you over the years and express gratitude. If you do these things, your relationship with God will be more than you ever dreamed. And truly, all things will work together for good.

People say it is so hard. I try with all my might, but I cannot keep myself on the straight and narrow. There is a secret to that. Realize, really come to grips with the fact that you cannot be good. There are 613 commands in the Old Testament. There are 1050 commands in the New Testament. The devil's district attorney is building a rap sheet against you and me for every one of our violations. The devil's demons have issued arrest warrants, and the demon minions are looking for us. The good news is, as Christians, our defense attorney has the power to issue complete pardons for all our wrongs. And He loves us and wants to issue the pardons!

There is no condemnation for those who are in Christ. Two things, though, when we are in Christ, we have a new nature that wants to please God. There needs to be evidence that we have that new nature. But we still have the old nature, and they war against each other. This means we want to do what God wants, but we will struggle against the old nature. Over time, we will get better, but our hope always must be in Him and not our behavior. Secondly, the fruit will come from those who have truly asked Christ to be their Savior. Fruit of changing character, fruit of intimacy with God, fruit of God's plan for you being worked out. In a truly converted person, fruit will grow and increase. So, if you have no desire to do what God wants, you must question where you truly are with Christ. Revisit it. Ask Him sincerely to forgive you and give you a heart that wants what He wants.

If you try to defeat the old nature in your own power, it will defeat you on a regular basis. Even then, there is no condemnation for those in Christ. God treats you as one of his children. He will discipline you, but that is a mark of truly being His child. Ask for forgiveness and keep going. You are forgiven, and all things work together for good for those who love God and are called according to His purpose.

C.S. Lewis said, "No man knows how bad he is until he has tried very hard to be good." Your hope and my hope are in the Cross, the Blood of Christ, and the power of the Holy Spirit. To win this battle, we need to thank God every day that He was willing to rescue us. Ask Him, every day, to keep you, provide for you, Shepard you, and give you eyes to see and ears to hear. Ask Him to fill you with the Spirit, anoint you with the Spirit, and baptize you with the Spirit. This transforms our mind. And because of this, more and more, we can strengthen the new man and weaken the old man.

Many people ask what is meant by the baptism of the Holy Spirit and how is different from being filled with the Spirit or anointed by the Spirit. If you take a cup and fill it with water, it is filled with water. If you pour water in the sink and dunk the cup, it is baptized in the water. If you pour water over the cup to separate it for special service, then it is anointed. The scripture clearly says we are to have all three. Acts 1:5 clearly says we are to be baptized by the Holy Spirit. This is for the power of God to be unleashed in our lives. Do not let old prejudices make you afraid. Just ask God and let Him do what He will. You will feel defeated pretty much forever until you rely on God as your source of everything.

No one has arrived at perfection. We are all tempted, and sometimes we do not do well. If we will own it, ask God to forgive us, then we can get up and going again, with deeper character being gained. He will take even our intentional mistakes and use them to rescue others and build His Kingdom. Failure to be what we want and who we want is part of the journey to maturity. Jesus's sacrifice on the cross is enough. Enough for your past, enough for your present, and enough for your future.

So here is the secret sauce of life: Call on God, Run to God, bow the knee to God, trust God in the days of light and in the days that are dark. Do all you can to seek Him with all your heart. Do all you can to develop a deep personal relationship with Him. Ask Him to want what He wants and see what He sees.

You will have an abundant life both here and in eternity. It is the secret sauce to peace, to joy, and to making your life count. When we really do this, we are "living what we believe"!

Here are some practical things that make a big difference. Keep a list of how God has done miracles for you, how He has delivered you, how He has answered prayer, how His way has worked things out for the best. The devil has come to kill, steal, and destroy. He specializes in discouragement. So, reminding ourselves of the truth of how faithful God has been builds our faith.

Be aware of how God speaks to you. He speaks in authentic corporate worship. He speaks in authentic private worship. He speaks in prayer. He speaks to you as you read His Word. He speaks to you in the community of others who truly hunger and thirst after God. He speaks in the books, the recordings, and videos of those who love God and are truly seeking Him. He will speak in a still, small voice when we are seeking Him with all our heart. He will speak in the context of your calling, mission, and the vision God has given for your life. He will speak in the context of the gifts, talents, and experience God has given you. He speaks through open and closed doors when we are seeking Him. He often will speak with an "ah ha" moment in a movie, a book, play, or TV program.

Still, in the context of seeking Him for guidance, He often will speak in dreams, visions, or life-after-death experiences. He proves His existence to you in creation and through your conscience. He speaks through prophecy, preaching, and the love of those who love Him. He speaks as we serve and love others. It is important for you when a course of action needs to be decided to get confirmation on multiple channels of how God will speak to you. The key is an authentic deep heart desire for His will. If you feel you may not be fully there, ask Him to give you that full-on devotion to His plan.

God does love you. He is for you. However, He is for what is best for you for eternity and for His plan for you on earth. He is not for what the world thinks you should do. He is not for what your old nature of the flesh wants to do. And He is not for the siren call of darkness that deceives us into thinking bad is good. He is everlastingly teaching us to trust Him in the dark. God does not want us to hedge our bets. Bet 100% on Him in every situation. God is always full-on in your life at every moment. He is never preoccupied with other things. Trust that He loves you. That He knows what to do. That He has the power to do it. And He will do what is best for you. Every time. No matter how bad it looks. He is for you. He is for you! He is for you!!

In closing, I would like to give you what God has burned into my soul, what "live what you believe" means. It has occurred to me fairly recently that His saying live what you believe may be related to my confession. When I was asked, "Are you ready for this manuscript to go to the publisher, I replied, I am betting everything on Christ. He is my Savior and Lord. So, God is saying if that is what you confess, then live it.

To do that, first, we must be authentic and transparent. God hates posers. Secondly, be what you say you are.

If you say you believe in forgiveness, then forgive. If you say you believe in seeking God will all your heart, then do it if you are not sure how that looks, pray, study, and be with those who love God. God will reveal it to you. If you claim to worship God, do it with all your heart. Go to worship events. Do it even if it costs you money. Make worship music the background noise of your life. Not music that is against God. Show up at church planning to meet with God in worship. If you say you love others, remember real love costs. Pay the price. If you say the Bible has the answers, let God speak to you daily from His Word. If you say you care about the lost, then pay the price to win their hearts. Demonstrate love and earn a place in their life to speak. If you say you believe, "show me your friends, and I'll show you your future," then do life only with those who hunger and thirst after God. You can be friendly with almost everyone. But doing life, being vulnerable, is reserved for the true followers of Christ. If you say you believe in eternal life, then eliminate the fear of death for yourself and those you love. If you say you believe in prayer, pray multiple times daily. Pray for those who love you, hate you, and are against you. Pray that God will help you with intimacy with Him. Pray for your calling and destiny. Pray that you will not fear. Pray for hope. Pray for assurance that you are a child of His. And for assurance that you truly are forgiven, redeemed, justified, and are being kept by the power of God. Pray to be forgiven. And talk to Him about all the issues of life every day.

Chapter 31.

Final Thoughts - Sherry

The Lord is always good. He is always loving and kind, and His faithfulness goes on and on to each succeeding generation. Psalm 100:5 (TLB)

Sometimes, when you are in the thick of problems, sickness, financial setbacks, business crises, or even day-to-day problems, we cannot seem to find the goodness of God. It can be very hard to trust in His goodness when you feel pain or see heartache all around you, or you feel like there is absolutely no way out of the situation you are in. But God is so good. When you look back, you can see His faithfulness.

Mike and I celebrated our twenty-fifth anniversary this year. Today, five of our six children are married to wonderful spouses. God-chosen spouses make a powerful union. They have given us thirteen precious Grands, as I like to call them. Mike and I have a rewarding relationship with all of them. As only God can do to redeem our mistakes and our lives making good on His promise in Romans 8:28. He will cause ALL things to work together for good to those who love the Lord and are called according to His purpose. Aimee and Melissa's half-sister, Kristin, reappeared in their lives. The sisters have reunited with each other. Kristin and her husband, whose name is Mike, have become Christians. They have two little girls. Kristin's mom reconciled with Aimee, Melissa, and me. Before Kristin's Grandma passed away, Kristin asked if I would write her grandma a card and let her know all was well between us. I did. She passed soon after she received the note. Not only is God faithful, but he is an Ephesians 3:20 God. Now to Him who is able to do immeasurably more than all we ask or imagine, according to His power that is at work within us. Never doubt the promises of God!

Chapter 32.

Final Thoughts - Mike

People who "live what they believe as a Christian" are the truly rich. And it is fully available to everyone. You do not need to be "full-time" in the ministry. You do not need authority. You do not need wealth or fame. You need a deep relationship with Jesus. The deepest theology takes us back to the start of our Christian journey. Believe God and trust in Him no matter what it looks like. Sherry and I know what we have written in this book is the heart of God and the path to the best life possible. Our hope and prayer is that the Holy Spirit will speak to you in a life-changing way. God's richest blessings on you!

Mike and Sherry Nickols

Mike Nickols, his Mom and Dad
Shirley, Jack and Mike Nickols

Mike Nickols 1969 Football picture

Indiana University SAE House before the fire, Bloomington IN

Sherry's Mom and Dad: Winston and Mildred Flynn

Sherry's Nana aka Drill Sergeant, Elsie Flynn

Mike and Sherry Nickols wedding 4/10/1997: Mike and Sherry Nickols
Judge Fran Gull, Allen County IN Courthouse

Aimee, Melissa and Kristi, Aimee, Melissa and Kristi; one of the last
times they would see her until adulthood

Serenade of the Seas, Royal Caribbean Ship for Barbados Adventure

Barbados Adventure Participants: Front Row, from left to right: Sherri Campbell, Cecily Campbell (Bill Campbell's daughter), Aimee, daughter, Jena (Matt's first wife), Sherry Nickols, Kelli Ferguson, Jill (Aimee's friend), Pam Pratt, Mike's sister, Renita Ellington, standing above Pam, Tour Driver, Melissa, daughter.

Top Row: Pastor Bill Campbell, then Sr. Pastor of Calvary Temple, Cory Nickols, Matt Nickols, Mike Nickols, Benny Ferguson, then Worship Pastor of Calvary Temple, Tyler Nickols, son, Mark Ellington, then Asst. Pastor, Calvary Temple, Dennis Pratt, brother-in-law, Rory Siren, son-in-law, holding Gabby Siren, Granddaughter.

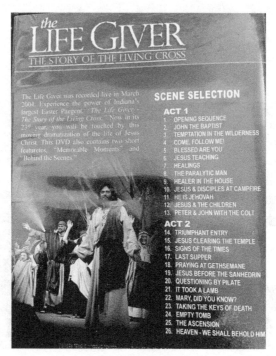

the LIFE GIVER
THE STORY OF THE LIVING CROSS

The Life Giver was recorded live in March 2004. Experience the power of Indiana's largest Easter Pageant, *The Life Giver - The Story of the Living Cross.* Now in its 23rd year, you will be touched by this moving dramatization of the life of Jesus Christ. This DVD also contains two short featurettes, "Memorable Moments" and "Behind the Scenes."

SCENE SELECTION

ACT 1
1. OPENING SEQUENCE
2. JOHN THE BAPTIST
3. TEMPTATION IN THE WILDERNESS
4. COME, FOLLOW ME!
5. BLESSED ARE YOU
6. JESUS TEACHING
7. HEALINGS
8. THE PARALYTIC MAN
9. HEALER IN THE HOUSE
10. JESUS & DISCIPLES AT CAMPFIRE
11. HE IS JEHOVAH
12. JESUS & THE CHILDREN
13. PETER & JOHN WITH THE COLT

ACT 2
14. TRIUMPHANT ENTRY
15. JESUS CLEARING THE TEMPLE
16. SIGNS OF THE TIMES
17. LAST SUPPER
18. PRAYING AT GETHSEMANE
19. JESUS BEFORE THE SANHEDRIN
20. QUESTIONING BY PILATE
21. IT TOOK A LAMB
22. MARY, DID YOU KNOW?
23. TAKING THE KEYS OF DEATH
24. EMPTY TOMB
25. THE ASCENSION
26. HEAVEN - WE SHALL BEHOLD HIM

Life Giver DVD Cover

Hillsong Conference in Sydney Australia

Nickols Family vacation 2007 5 years after the heart attacks at Tween Waters Captiva Island, FL: Front Row seated: Gabby Siren leaning on her

Mom, Melissa Siren, Sherry holding Granddaughter, Olivia James (Aimee),

Mike holding Grandson, Micah (Matt),Amy Nickols (Matt's wife), Anna Rose, Granddaughter, (Matt).

Back Row standing: Aimee James pregnant with Avari, Brad James, son-in-law, Rory Siren, holding Grandson, Luke, Tyler Nickols, Craig Nickols, Cory Nickols, Matt Nickols.

Nickols Family vacation (those who could make it) to Hawaii, 2021, twenty years after Mike's heart attacks. We love to laugh! Olivia and Avari James in the front row, all grown up.

Luke's 2022 Graduation Picture: Left to right: Natalie Nickols with Jane in front, Tyler Nickols, Melissa Siren, Luke Siren, Avari James. Back row: Rory Siren, Olivia James, Gabby Siren with Levi Nickols, Will Nickols in front of her, Aimee James, Brad James behind Aimee, Sherry Nickols, Mike Nickols behind Sherry.

Mike and Sherry Nickols at the New York Yankees Spring Training 2022

James Family (Aimee) Avari, Far Left, Aimee, 2nd Left, Brad, 2nd Right, Olivia, Far Right

Matt Nickols Family Anna Rose, Far Left, Amy holding Oliver "Ollie" 2nd left, Matt, Middle, Everly, 2nd Right, Micah, Far Right

Rory Siren, Far Left, Melissa Siren 2nd Left, Luke Siren, 2nd right, Gabby Siren, Far Right

Xavier Nickols Far Left, Craig Nickols 2nd left, Kristin Nickols, 2nd Right holding Stella Nickols.

Mike Nickols, Left and Cory Nickols, Right.

Will Nickols, Far Left, Natalie Nickols, 2nd left holding Levi Nickols,
Tyler Nickols 2nd right holding Jane Nickols.

Paul/Jackie Johnson, Far Left Mike
and Sherry Nickols 2nd lefty
Dennis and Pam Pratt 2nd right
Jeff and Shelli Nickols Far right

Sherry's sister, Karen Sterman on horseback; Sherry (wearing helmet)
and Karen Sterman, Sherry's older sister in green vest.

Made in the USA
Monee, IL
02 October 2023

43868032R00103